What Are They Saying about the Book of Revelation?

by
John J. Pilch

see p. 47

p. 53

p. 59

D1295919

PAULIST PRESS
New York, N.Y./Ramsey, N.J.

Library of Congress
Catalog Card Number: 78-58954

ISBN: 0-8091-2126-3

Published by Paulist Press
Editorial Office: 1865 Broadway, New York, N.Y. 10023
Business Office: 545 Island Road, Ramsey, N.J. 07446

Printed and bound in the
United States of America

Contents

65137

Preface

In the late 1950's I encountered a very stimulating teacher. One day he told us the story of how, ever anxious to broaden his horizons and feed his intellectual curiosity, he had resolved early in his career to study in depth a different subject each year. Once he tried to unravel the secrets of the Book of Revelation by reading all the commentaries he could gather in languages familiar to him. The year-long study did not yield much clarity of insight, but certain segments of the book, and notably Revelation 21:15-21, so intrigued him that he resolved for the subsequent year to study gemology.

An exegete might wish that he had been inspired to undertake similar study of other books in the Bible, but considering the kinds of commentaries available to my teacher and the attitudes prevailing in Catholic scholarship at that time, one cannot be surprised if his study of Revelation did no more than inspire him to study precious stones.

True, Pope Pius XII already in 1943 had issued a landmark encylical, *Divino Afflante Spiritu* (Inspired by the Divine Spirit) which outlined a new direction for Catholic biblical scholars. Besides demanding that they study biblical texts in the original languages and make new translations, the Pope insisted

that scholars should pursue above all the literal sense
of these texts. History, archeology, and the study of
literary forms were singled out as indispensable aids
in this quest. "Let him be convinced," said the Pon-
tiff, "that this part of his office cannot be neglected
without serious detriment to Catholic exegesis" (38).

There was much catching up for Catholic scholars to do with the uninhibited Protestant scholarship
of the preceding 50 years, but they accepted the
challenge and pursued their biblical research vig-
orously along these lines. There was much to be
done, and major interests of the times forced them to
focus special attention on Genesis, creation and evolution, the relationship of science to the Bible, and
new ways of studying the Gospels. Some scholars
continued their research on the Book of Revelation,
but at the popular level, fundamentalistic approaches generally prevailed. Most people continued to read the book as a collection of predictions
telling the identity of the anti-Christ, describing the
time and method in which the world would end, and
indicating exactly how many would be saved.

Then in 1962 came the Second Vatican Council;
and three years later, its Decree on Divine Revelation repeated and further developed the exhortation
of Pius XII:

Those who search out the intention of the sacred
writers must, among other things, have regard
for "literary forms." For truth is proposed and
expressed in a variety of ways, depending on
whether a text is a history of one kind or an-

other, or whether its form is that of prophecy, poetry or some other type of speech. The interpreter must investigate what meaning the sacred writer intended to express and actually expressed in particular circumstances as he used contemporary literary forms in accordance with the situation of his own time and culture. For the correct understanding of what the sacred author wanted to assert, due attention must be paid to the customary and characteristic styles of perceiving, speaking, and narrating which prevailed at the time of the sacred writer, and to the customs men normally followed at that period in their everyday dealings with one another (12).

This document was promulgated on November 18, 1965, twenty-two years after Pius' encyclical.

The best scholarship of the period was already reflecting these principles. Feine-Behm-Kümmel's scholarly *Introduction to the New Testament*[1] affirmed:

The Apocalypse is a book of its time, written out of its time and for its time, not for the distant generations of the future or even of the end time. It is an occasional writing as much so as are the epistles of the NT, and which therefore, as a matter of principle, should be understood in relationship to the history of its time.[1]

Thus, the Second Vatican Council added new emphasis to Pius' earlier exhortations. It urged the bishops "to give the faithful entrusted to them suitable instruction in the *right use* of the divine books" (#25). This clearly required a level and kind of popularization that did not previously exist. Yet, happily, Catholic scholars were already anticipating this very task. In 1962, the Liturgical Press, Collegeville, Minn., published William Heidt's commentary on *The Book of the Apocalypse* in its series, *New Testament Reading Guide*, initiated two years earlier for use by the laity. With brevity and in plain language he interprets Revelation, against the background of its time, just as scientific scholarship and papal instruction suggest. Contemporary examples of this same kind of popularization are the article, "Revelation," in *The New World Dictionary-Concordance to the New American Bible* (New York: World Publishing Co., 1970). a source book written by priest-biblical-scholars in Rome, Italy; and Elisabeth Schuessler Fiorenza's booklet, *The Apocalypse* (Chicago, Ill.: Franciscan Herald Press, 1976).

In this present book I (1) present a review of scholarship on apocalyptic in general as it has developed in the last two decades; (2) examine scholarship on the Book of Revelation in particular; (3) discuss the prophetic-apocalyptic character and message of Revelation; and (4) evaluate the popular understanding and liturgical usage of the book. This is meant to present in a nutshell what they are saying about the Book of Revelation today.

1
Biblical Scholarship and Apocalyptic

"This is the revelation God gave to Jesus Christ, that he might show his servants what must happen very soon. He made it known by sending his angel to his servant John . . ." This opening sentence in the Book of Revelation contains a Greek word, *apokalypsis* (that is, revelation, uncovering, removing a veil), from which the English words, apocalypse and apocalyptic, are derived. The Book of Revelation has sometimes been known as the Apocalypse. Literature resembling the Apocalypse and likewise claiming to unveil divine secrets about the end-time is classified as apocalyptic, an adjective also used to characterize the four centuries extending from 200 BC to 200 AD in which these writings flourished. The modern, non-biblical usage of the word apocalyptic is generally directed to describing people, literature, or movements obsessed with end-time concerns.

Even in the age that it was written, the literature was baffling. For all its claim to make known what must happen soon, its imagery was bizarre; its theological themes differed from traditional, acceptable, or expected themes; and its message was often obscure within a code whose key was not immediately evident or widely known. Small wonder then that of all the representative literature that was composed, only the Book of Daniel was accepted into the Jewish scriptures, and only the Book of Revelation was accepted into the Christian scriptures, though traces of apocalyptic style and themes can be identified and isolated in other scripture passages.

The popularity of the literature relates chiefly to the mood of an age or the circumstances of regions and people. In times of distress when human effort seems futile for working desirable changes, interest in apocalyptic literature rises as people seek relief from suffering, either in messages of comfort or in the calculation of signs and portents heralding an end to the present distress. Conversely, when times do improve, and the world does not end but goes on, interest in the literature declines. As one scholar has observed, the literature has never been consistently popular in teaching or preaching, nor has it been regularly and extensively used in spiritual direction and meditation.

Unquestionably, the puzzling character of the literature and the ambiguity of its form and symbolism, which allows for varieties of far-fetched interpretation, have contributed to its relative neglect. The last twenty years of critical, biblical scholarship, however, have yielded landmark results that have faciliated study and appreciation of apocalyptic literature in general and the Book of Revelation in particular. While much more research remains to be done in order to resolve the many questions still unanswered, the current state of knowledge deserves to be better known in order that the popular reading and study of Revelation may begin to incorporate the firm and generally accepted achievements of scholarship. In this chapter, therefore, the work of three key biblical scholars will be reviewed: D.S. Russell, Klaus Koch, and Paul D. Hanson.

The Puzzle of Apocalyptic Literature

The British scholar, David Symes Russell, published a book in 1960 entitled: *Between the Testaments.*[2] Here he sketched the historical situation in which apocalyptic literature arose and briefly treated some of its basic themes such as the expectation of a redeemer figure and resurrection. Russell's concern was to help fill a gap which existed in many views of the Bible that often leapt from Isaiah, Jeremiah, and Ezekiel, past Daniel and the Maccabees, to Jesus. Granting the popular division of the Bible into Old and New Testaments, there is a tendency on the part of scholars to specialize in one or the other segment but Russell was one of those who specialized in the writings of that significant space of time separating the extant literature of the two distinct areas. He studied the considerable body of literature composed by Jews and later by Christians of this era in the firm conviction that such study was important for understanding the relationship of the two testaments and their literature.

Four years later, in 1964, Russell published a fuller presentation of his researches and investigations into the intertestamental era (as it is known) under the title: *The Method and Message of Jewish Apocalyptic*.[3] His work was then and continues now to be cited and used as a point of orientation by all who would read apocalyptic literature with profit. Nevertheless, his book can be as frustrating as it attempted to be enlightening. Consider, for example, his comprehensive listing of the characteristics of apocalyptic: transcendentalism; mythology; cosmological orientation, pessimistic historical view; dualism; division of time into eras; two eras; numerology; pseudo-ecstacy; artificial claims of inspiration; pseudonymity; esotericism; unity of history; conceptions of cosmic history which treats of heaven and earth; notion of primordiality; speculation on the source of evil in the world; conflict between light and darkness, good and evil, God and Satan; Son of Man; life after death; and individualism. The terms are precise but technical and generally unfamiliar and undecipherable to the general reader. The list is indeed comprehensive, but also unwieldy if one attempts to use it as a tool for better understanding apocalyptic literature. Russell's results were welcome but needed better organization to be of general utility.

Apocalyptic: A Literary Type

In 1972, the German scholar Klaus Koch's 1969 research work was published under the English title: *The Rediscovery of Apocalyptic*.[4] Koch reviewed the ups and downs of research on the topic throughout this century and succeeded in putting a perspective to his results that had eluded earlier scholars. Basing himself on the Hebrew and Aramaic apocalyptic literature—Daniel, 1 Henoch, 2 Baruch, IV Ezra, and the Apocalypse of Abraham—he was able to distinguish between apocalyptic as a literary type and apocalyptic as a frame of mind reflecting particularly distressing historical situations.

Six characteristics can be singled out in apocalyptic literature: great discourse cycles; effect of the vision or audition on the seer; the content: paranaetic discourse or legends; pseudonymity; mythical imagery rich in symbolism; and a composite character. It should be noted that these characteristics do not necessarily constitute a discrete apocalyptic literary form. Rather, they are the striking characteristics of the literature in which apocalyptic visionaries appear to have preferred to express themselves. The characteristics are uniform enough and repeated sufficiently often to suggest literary patterns. A review of these characteristics as they are found in the Book of Daniel can shed some light on the Christian apocalypse, the Book of Revelation.

To begin with, apocalyptic literature contains

great discourse cycles which report discussions between the seer and his angel-interpreter. In Daniel
7:2, for instance, he begins to describe his vision:
"In the vision I saw during the night, suddenly the
four winds of heaven stirred up the great sea etc.,"
and then in Daniel 7:16, he "approached one of those
present and asked him what all this meant in truth;
in answer, he made known to me the meaning of the
things." Sometimes the discourse cycle centers on
visions as just illustrated, and at other times it centers on things that are heard, as in Daniel 9. Often
the words "see," "lo," "behold" (in Hebrew) begin
these discourses.

Similar features mark the Book of Revelation.
"I heard behind me a piercing voice like the sound
of a trumpet, which said, 'Write on a scroll what
you now see and send it to the seven churches...' I
turned around to see whose voice it was that spoke
to me. When I did so I saw seven lampstands of gold
and among the lampstands one like a Son of Man
. . ." (1:10-12). After the visions of the beast and the
harlot in Chapter 17, the angel says to John: "Why
are you so taken aback? I will explain to you the
symbolism of the woman and of the seven-headed
and ten horned beast carrying her" (17:7).

A second characteristic in the literature is a
description of the effect of the vision or the audition
on the seer. Koch admits that it is difficult to decide
whether the effect is simply literary, or indeed quite
real. The formalized phraseology and the sheer
number of visions and auditions make one wonder
whether the statement is only for literary purposes.

"I, Daniel, found my spirit anguished within its sheath of flesh, and I was terrified by the visions of my mind" (7:15) or again, "I, Daniel, was greatly terrified by my thoughts, and my face blanched, but I kept the matter to myself" (7:28).

The same effect is noted in Revelation, but not as frequently as in Daniel. Commenting on his initial vision and audition, John concludes: "When I caught sight of him I fell down at his feet as though dead." Curiously, two other instances of reaction to visions and/or auditions are postures of worship: 19:10 and 22:8.

A third characteristic of the literature is the nature of its message. The visions specifically appear to provide advice on a pattern for living through and surviving the distress in which the community finds itself at the present time. In Daniel, this aspect of the message is found in the first six chapters which relate the experiences of the Jewish youth, Daniel, and his friends at a non-Jewish court in the service of a non-Jewish king. The legends or tales demonstrate how one can be faithfully observant of one's religious obligations in a foreign, if not hostile, environment.

This kind of story was, of course, familiar to Jewish readers. Joseph in the court of the Pharaoh, and Esther and Mordecai in the Persian Kingdom under Ahasuerus related how faithfully observant Jews who found themselves in threatening circumstances would—by holding fast to their traditions—experience final deliverance. The same message is intended in Daniel. Perhaps one reason why these stories, which seem to have had an earlier existence, were repeated in Daniel is that they contain dreams and visions and would thus relate quite appropriately to the extended visions of Daniel in the later chapters of the book.

In the Book of Revelation, the letters to the seven churches seem to serve the same purpose as the stories in Daniel. The letters offer advice and encouragement on how to remain faithful in the face of adversity and especially in view of the imminent distress. Both the letters of Revelation and the tales in Daniel relate to the lengthy hortatory speeches found in other apocalyptic literature serving the same purposes. From this perspective, it can be appreciated why apocalyptic literature has often been characterized as a kind of "resistance" literature.

A fourth characteristic of this literature listed by Koch actually distinguishes Revelation from all the rest: namely, pseudonymity. Jewish apocalyptic literature is generally ascribed to a worthy ancient, e.g., Moses, Henoch, Daniel, who is supposed to have had visions in his time relative to a given period of time centuries later. The material frequently mirrors inaccuracies about the period of its alleged origins (or its vocabulary is from an obviously later period), while the period for which its message is intended is remarkably accurate. Thus, Daniel claims as its author a Jewish youth taken early to Babylon where he lived at least until 538 BC. Careful analysis of the book itself, however, reveals that it was definitely composed by someone living in 167 to 164 BC and experiencing those very events. By hiding, as it were, behind the name of a venerable ancient, the real author hoped to accomplish two things: one, to lend prestige and authority to his writing; and two, to heighten the impact of his present advice by reporting successful fulfillment of prophecies presumably made centuries earlier and known to the readers as fulfilled in their past history.

The Book of Revelation, however, is definitely not a pseudonymous composition. The author reveals his name repeatedly (1:1, 4, 9; 22:8), ranks himself among the prophets (1:3; 22:9), and is presumably very familiar to his addressees with whom he shares the sufferings of the present distress (1:9). Judging from the forceful tone of the letters he addresses to the churches (2:1-3:22), he is well known to the Christians of Asia and seems to enjoy uncontested authority.

It has been suggested that in view of the Christian belief in Jesus as Messiah and in his imminent second coming, there was no further need for pseudonymous authorship. What was desired—and provided!—was a clear interpretation of the present situation, an unravelling of the meaning of the present oppression and the determination or revelation of the anticipated solution to the current problems.

Fifthly, Jewish apocalyptic literature is definitely characterized by a wealth of mythical imagery rich in symbolism. Israel, for instance, is frequently represented in the Jewish scriptures under the guise of a symbol such as a vine (Is 5) or a lion (Num 23:24; 24:9). Its enemies are often portrayed

as waters (Jer 47:2; Is 8:7) or beasts as in Jer 5:6:
"Therefore lions from the forest slay them, wolves
of the desert ravage them, leopards keep watch
round their cities: all who come out are torn to
pieces for their crimes and their numerous rebel-
lions." Apocalyptic imagery turns these same
figures grotesque, as in Daniel 7:5: "And after this I
looked and saw another beast, like a leopard; on its
back were four wings like those of a bird, and it had
four heads."

The enemy-beasts in Revelation are equally
grotesque: "Then I saw a wild beast come out of the
sea with ten horns and seven heads; and on its
horns were ten diadems and on its heads blasphe-
mous names. The beast I saw was like a leopard, but
it had paws like a bear and the mouth of a lion"
(13:1-2). Indeed, the Book of Revelation is heavily
laden with symbolism drawn particularly from the
prophetic tradition.

An understanding of this symbolism renders
the book subject to more reasonable and plausible
interpretation. It is tantamount to having a key to
crack a code. For instance, a woman represents a
people (12:1ff) or a city (17:1ff); horns point to
power (5:6; 12:3), and most especially the power of
a dynasty (13:1; 17:3ff). Clearly, wings would indicate mobility (4:8; 12:14), and eyes, signify knowledge (1:14; 2:18; 4:6; 5:6). The blast of trumpets
would suggest superhuman divine voices (1:10;
8:2ff), while the familiar sharp sword symbolizes
the Word of God that both judges and punishes
(1:16; 2:12, 16; 19:15; 19:21).

Colors also play symbolic roles: purple is associated with luxury and kingship (17:4; 18:12; 18:16); black relates to death (6:5, 12); and of course white demonstrates joy, at times the joy of victory (1:14; 2:17; 3:4f, 18; 4:4; 6:11; 7:9, 13; 19:11, 14). White robes characterize the world of glory (6:11; 7:9, 13; 22:14). Palms in Revelation as in antiquity are signs of triumph (7:9), while crowns patently represent dominion and kingship (2:10; 3:11; 4:10; 6:2; 12:1; 14:14).

Symbolic numbers play an especially significant role in the Book of Revelation. Seven (used 54 times) signifies fullness or perfection; twelve (used 23 times) recalls the twelve tribes of Israel and together with its multiples suggest that the people of God has achieved its promised end-time perfection. Four (used 16 times) is indicative of the whole world, or the universality of any statement, or element. Three and a half (half of seven) points to incompleteness, imperfection, failure. Six, one less than seven, is an exasperating failure, while a triple six (13:18) is an unquestionable failure.

Koch's final characteristic of apocalyptic literature is its composite character. Daniel, for instance, contains Hebrew (1; 8-12); Aramaic (2-7); and Greek (13-14) segments. Koch believes that this feature points to the lengthy tradition behind the book.

That this characteristic can be attributed to the Book of Revelation is debatable. There are no significant language differences as in Daniel to signal varied "editions," but some scholars have argued that the book is composed of discrete and distinct literary units deriving from different persecutions, or other contexts. Josephine Massyngberde Ford has taken up a form of this position in her recent Anchor Bible Commentary on the Book of Revelation.[5] But other scholars insist on the literary unity of the text and ascribe apparent inconsistencies in the composition to the general nature of apocalyptic. Since there does not exist a unanimous position on this subject, it will have to wait—as will many other questions in Revelation—for further investigations of scholarship.

Apocalyptic: A Frame of Mind

Koch further pointed out that the literary characteristics he identified appeared particularly adapted to reflect an apocalyptic frame of mind or attitude. He listed these aspects of such a frame of mind: there is an urgent expectation of the imminent end of earthly existence; this end will be a catastrophe of cosmic proportions; for this reason, the duration of the world has been predetermined; human effort which is now useless must yield to angelic and demonic efforts; after the catastrophe a new salvation will appear, which must derive from the throne of God, by means, of course, of a mediator. Glory will characterize the final state.

There is no doubt that the literature gives a clear impression of urgent expectation of the impending overthrow of all earthly conditions in the immediate future. The last three verses of Chapter

12 in the Book of Daniel give vibrant expression to such an expectation: "From the time that the daily sacrifice is abolished and the horrible abomination set up, there shall be one thousand two hundred and ninety days . . ." This is a patently calculable reality of the calendar. Those who witnessed the sacrilegious deeds of Antiochus Epiphanes (the event referred to in the text) would take consolation in counting the finite number of days until final deliverance. But when the time elapsed and nothing changed, it appears that the author added this comment: "Blessed is the man who has patience and perseveres until the one thousand three hundred and thirty five days." When this, too, passed uneventfully, the final advice was written: "Go, take your rest, you shall rise for your reward at the end of days" (whenever it shall come to pass) (Dan 12:11-13).

This sense of urgency is no less clear in Revelation. John claims to report "what must happen very soon" (1:1; 22:6), for "the appointed time is near" (1:3; 22:10). In describing the meaning of the beast, John writes: "The ten horns you saw represent ten kings who have not yet been crowned; they will possess royal authority along with the beast, but only for an hour" (17:12; see 18:10,17,19).

A second element of this frame of mind is that the end appears as a vast cosmic catastrophe. Daniel notes: "Then the kingship and dominion and majesty of all the kingdoms under the heavens shall be given to the holy people of the most high, whose kingdom shall serve and obey him" (Dan 7:27).

Revelation's references to the four corners of the earth (7:1 and 20:8) indicate the worldwide dimensions of what must take place, while the references to open heavens from which various elements can be viewed or descend, as, for instance, the new Jerusalem "coming down out of heaven from God" (3:12; 21:2, 10) also indicate the cosmic dimension of what must soon come to pass. The point is that what appears to be a small human concern has repercussions not only throughout the entire earth but in the heavens as well.

The urgent expectation of the end leads the apocalyptic-minded individual to believe that the time of this world is fixed into segments, predetermined in duration. In Daniel, the angel Gabriel explains to the seer that it will take "seventy weeks" of years before deliverance shall take place, and then proceeds to explain this strange calculation (9:24ff). Of course, all these figures are intended to be understood as approximate, even if the affirmation seems to be calendar-perfect. The Book of Revelation similarly speaks of such predeterminations, though in somewhat restricted terms. It tells of a time, and times, and a half a time (12:14; see also Dan 12:7); 1260 days (11:3; 12:6); 42 months (11:2; 13:5)—all indications for the time period of three and a half years, a number half of seven, indicative of short duration and signifying imperfection, incompletion, and non-fulfillment.

Beyond this factor, in view of the actual experience of centuries-long futility to human effort, it is understandable why angels and demons begin to play a large role in apocalyptic literature. In Daniel, the angel Gabriel (10:5; cf. 9:21) serves as an interpreter and explains the visions to Daniel. In other activities, however, Gabriel is impeded by "the prince of the Kingdom of Persia" (10:13) who is actually the "guardian angel of that nation," until Michael, one of the "chief princes" (10:13) and the "great prince guardian" of Israel (12:12) comes to his assistance. Thus does all meaningful activity begin to take place on a supra-terrestrial sphere.

A similar outlook is evident in Revelation. For instance, the letters to the churches are directed to the angels or presiding spirits of the seven churches. The reference most probably refers to the guardian angels, i.e., the celestial counterparts of these communities. They are judged to share in the responsibility for and participate in the destiny of these communities which they represent as well as guard. The fact that Christ holds them in his right hand shows that he is the Lord of these communities and that they are under his protection.

The war in heaven between Michael and his angels against the dragon and his angels (Rev 12:7ff) demonstrates the belief that what happens on earth no longer matters. Everything is decided by otherworldly beings who are now clearly in charge. The good angels interfere in history so as to promote the welfare of their given nation. Earthly history is no longer a product of human activities, but rather reflects the models which the visionaries see. Of course, in the future, barriers between here and the other world will vanish, and those who remain faithful will join the good angels and shine like stars in heaven (Dan 12:3). In Revelation, those who survive will become inhabitants of the New Jerusalem descended from heaven (Rev 22). Thus, it is clear why the salvation anticipated is paradisiacal in nature.

Further, the apocalyptic frame of mind believes that ultimately deliverance must come from the throne of God, although through a mediator. In Daniel 7:13, the one like a Son of Man ascends the throne, and in 7:14 the kingdom of God becomes visible on earth. The mysterious one like a son of man is sometimes human (e.g., 7:13) but again, the mediator may appear to be angelic (12:1).

In a similar vein, the throne is a central image in the Book of Revelation. After all, the entire book describes the conflict between the reign of God, Jesus, and his followers on the one hand, and the kingdom of the Beast and Babylon on the other. In chapter 4 God sits like a great king on his throne surrounded by his court. Jesus, because he is victorious, has a share in the reign of his Father. His title to such cosmic, heavenly kingship is the fact that in his death he has ransomed Christians from every tribe and tongue and nation and has made them into a kingdom and rendered them priests to God (see 5:9-10). In their present steadfast endurance, Christians witness to God's rule on earth and will share actively in kingship in the future (5:10; 20:6; 22:5). The final stage shall be glory, as in Daniel 12:3 and Revelation 21-22.

To sum up, Koch's distinction between

apocalyptic as a set of literary characteristics and apocalyptic as a frame of mind has been widely acclaimed as insightful and very useful for coming to grips with all the literature described as apocalyptic. In this review of his results, relationships with the Book of Revelation have demonstrated both the similarities as well as the differences between Jewish apocalyptic literature and Revelation.

The frame of mind described by Koch is understandable if one reflects even very briefly on the history of Israel. The experience of a magnificent era under King David who united the tribes into a nation and helped it become a power on the world-scene was given a certain dimension of permanence in the oracle pronounced by Nathan, the prophet, to the king: "Your house and your kingdom shall endure forever before me; your throne shall stand firm forever" (2 Sam 7:16). Imagine the disappointment when shortly after David's death during the reign of his son, Solomon, dissension grew and resulted in a split kingdom upon Solomon's death. This internal division was followed by Assyrian engulfment of the Northern Kingdom (Israel) in 721 BC and the Babylonian conquest of the Southern Kingdom (Judah) in 587 BC. Babylonian domination was successively replaced by Persian, Greek, and finally Roman rule, while Israel's hopes, based on the promises to Abraham and David, progressively deteriorated. It was this sense of futility that marked the apocalyptic period (200 BC to 200 AD) and gave birth to the apocalyptic frame of mind.

Apocalyptic: A View of History

While the thumbnail sketch of history which gave birth to apocalyptic has been generally known and accepted by scholars, it took the researches of a young Harvard scholar, Paul D. Hanson, to deepen and sharpen this understanding. In 1971, the world-renowned scholarly French-language biblical periodical, *Études Bibliques* published by the famous Dominican Biblical School of Jerusalem (the *École Biblique*) broke a more than seventy-year-old tradition and published the first English language article ever to appear on its pages. That article, written by Hanson, was entitled: "Jewish Apocalyptic against its Near-Eastern Environment."[6] The editorial judgment clearly indicated that the article was a major breakthrough in scholarship in an area of biblical study that had long eluded clarification.

That same year, in the United States, the popular biblical quarterly, *Interpretation*, published a companion piece by the same author entitled: "Old Testament Apocalyptic Re-examined."[7] The articles together presented an understanding of apocalyptic which made excellent sense of the evidence and opened new paths toward understanding apocalyptic literature. Hanson's full-length development of these ideas in book form finally appeared in 1975 under the title, *The Dawn of Apocalyptic.*[8] The book has been well received by critical scholarly reviewers. Raymond E. Brown, a biblical scholar and the only American member of the Pontifical Biblical

Commission, called it a "major contribution to the whole question of apocalyptic," adding that this book might "help those of us who struggle against simplistic attempts to remove apocalyptic eschatology from the ken of the historical Jesus".

The key to understanding Hanson's insight lies in three interrelated concepts: plain history, real politics, and human instrumentality. Hanson took up the comparisons familiar to many biblical scholars, comparisons between the prophets and the apocalyptic writers, and focused on these three interrelated concepts. Such a comparison clearly differentiates the prophets from the apocalypticists. The prophets were very interested in plain history, often engaged in real politics (some were court prophets), and believed in and urged human activity to remedy basic political problems. Apocalyptic writers, on the other hand, saw no purpose in plain history anymore, concluded that real politics were obviously unfavorable and could not be changed—at least not by humans, and thus were led to give up all interest in human effort to resolve dilemmas and unpleasant political life-situations. They turned instead to angels and demons and interventions by intermediaries with the ultimate salvation deriving from decisive intervention by God himself.

Previous scholars often spoke of a certain discontinuity between prophecy and apocalyptic based on the differences just noted. Hanson, however, believes that what appears to be discontinuity is in reality a development of prophecy into apocalyptic.

And this development is part of a broader, centuries-long development, of a fundamental tension between vision and reality, myth and history.

By vision Hanson understands an outlook that believes anything and everything of importance takes place on supra-terrestrial levels—in heaven—among the gods. Events on earth merely reflect that. Reality, on the other hand, refers to the arena of human existence and human efforts which determine the course and events of life on earth. Myth is the literary category in which vision as just described is expressed, while history is the literary category in which the record of human efforts and their outcome is noted.

Applying these insights to prophecy and apocalyptic as two phenomena in the Bible, Hanson has developed two very precise definitions.[9] According to him, prophecy is the "announcement to the nation of the divine plans for Israel and the world which the prophet, with his insight into Yahweh's divine council, has witnessed unfolding within the covenant relationship between Yahweh and Israel. These plans the prophet proceeds to translate into the terms of plain history, real politics, and human instrumentality." In other words, the prophet interprets for the king and people how God's plans will be accomplished within their own nation's history as well as within the history of the world.

Apocalyptic, he describes as "the disclosure (usually esoteric in nature) to the elect of the prophetic vision of Yahweh's sovereignty (including his future dealings with his people, the inner secrets of the cosmos, etc.) which vision the visionaries have ceased to translate into the terms of plain history, real politics, and human instrumentality because of a pessimistic view of reality growing out of the bleak post-exilic conditions in which the visionary group found itself, conditions seeming unsuitable to them as a context for the envisioned restoration of God's people."

To illustrate this contrast, it suffices to reflect on the classical prophet Isaiah. In Chapter 6 of the book bearing his name, Isaiah reports the inaugural or commissioning vision in which God appoints him to be his spokesman. He is instructed to deliver a message to the nation. In the next chapter, Isaiah is portrayed delivering his message: he boldly addresses the king, presenting the will of God for the circumstances, and when the king demurs (because he has already taken other political steps), Isaiah firmly announces that God's will is the better course of action and indeed imminent history will bear it out. Isaiah clearly speaks in the context of plain history, real politics, and human instrumentality.

How different is the message of Daniel. There, Daniel is the recipient of visions and explanations, but is not instructed to share them with anyone. Indeed, he is advised to seal up the message. "Go Daniel," he said, "because the words are to be kept secret and sealed until the end of time" (Dan 12:9). All important activity is carried out by the angels or princes of the nations. Human effort no longer has any effectiveness. Daniel illustrates the apocalyptic who is giving up on plain history, real politics, and human instrumentality.

The contrast posited here by Hanson cannot be viewed in isolation from the complete process of evolution of which it is a part. Even in the biblical literature alone—though he studies ancient near eastern literature in general as well—there is a process of thought-development that moves from pure vision (e.g., Ex 15:3-4 where God alone acts) to a healthy tension between vision and reality as evidenced in Isaiah and the other prophets, moving back toward pure vision as in Daniel and the other apocalyptic literature.

While he did not include Revelation in his work, Hanson's insights do improve the understanding of this book of the Bible. While obviously strongly colored by apocalyptic imagery and frame of mind, it nevertheless bears the unmistakable marks of prophecy. It is probably fair to say that Revelation marks a certain slippage from the healthy tension between prophecy and apocalyptic to something closer to the latter.

Summary

This chapter has focused on the research in apocalyptic that has broadened understanding and appreciation of the literature as well as the historical period in which it flourished. D.S. Russell's attempts at characterizing the literature were refined by Koch's distinction between apocalyptic as a literary type with distinct literary characteristics and apocalyptic as a frame of mind that expressed itself in a recognizable and discrete literary format. Hanson's focus on plain history, real politics, and human instrumentality not only helped to sharply distinguish prophecy and apocalyptic, but also helped situate both phenomena on an evolutionary line of development in the literature of the ancient Near East.

Though little of this research dealt with the Book of Revelation as such, continued application of the basic insights to the Christian work contributes to a better understanding of that book. In addition, it has set the stage for renewed research in the Book of Revelation and it is that aspect which we now turn to consider.

2
Biblical Scholarship and the Book of Revelation

The scholarly *Introduction to the New Testament* by Feine-Behm-Kümmel and other similar introductions generally summarize the opinions held by the majority of scholars on various biblical topics. Regarding the relationships of the Book of Revelation to the Jewish apocalypses, he observes:

Primitive Christianity was strongly influenced by apolcalyptic conceptions, which above all refer to the inbreaking of God's kingdom and the parousia of Christ. In Jesus' eschatological words, and in the expectation of the end by Paul and I and II John, resound thoughts of the Book of Daniel and of later Jewish apocalypticism. Mark 13 and parallels; 1 Thess. 4:15-17; 1 Thess 2:1-12; 1 Cor 15:20-28; II Cor 5:1ff; 12:4; Hebrews 12:22ff are signs that Christianity soon independently used and developed apocalyptic conceptions. Later the Christians went even further and created a Christian apocalyptic literature, either by revising Jewish apocalypses in a Christian direction (e.g., II

(IV) Ezra, Testaments of the 12 Patriarchs, Ascension of Isaiah, Christian Sybillines) or by composing new apocalypses (before the middle of the second century: Apocalypse of Peter, Shepherd of Hermas). The earliest and most significant apocalyptic work from Christian hands is the Apocalypse of John.[10]

Of course, not all scholars agree with this entire statement. While admitting that Revelation is indeed distinctive, some have maintained that Jesus could not be the inspiration or source for apocalyptic traces or ideas in any part of the New Testament writings. It took a vigorous debate on this idea, as well as a gradual unfolding of the investigations on the community at Qumrân and its literature, to promote increased appreciation for the pervasiveness of apocalyptic outlooks in the first century of the Christian era. This chapter will briefly review the debate on Jesus and apocalyptic as well as the story of Qumrân to provide some perspective for understanding what modern scholars have been saying about the Book of Revelation.

Jesus and Apocalyptic

Around the turn of the century, the famous polymath Albert Schweitzer published a monumental book entitled, *The Quest for the Historical Jesus*. In it he surveys and summarizes the studies seeking a true picture of the historical Jesus and judges their conclusion that Jesus was mainly an ethical teacher to be generally unsupported by the New Testament evidence. What Schweitzer proposed is that Jesus was truly characterized by an apocalyptic, end-time orientation in his life as well as in his teachings. The Jesus of the Gospels is a heroic figure, noble but deluded in that he convinced himself that he was the messiah. The message he offered was that the world was about to come to an end. When that did not occur, nor was there any indication that it would, he willingly brought about his death in an effort to bring on the end-time.

Though few scholars accepted the details of Schweitzer's conclusions, there was general agreement that more attention should be given to the apocalyptic background and framework of Jesus' teachings. In 1960, however, Professor Ernst Käsemann published a paper entitled, "The Beginnings of Christian Theology," in which he declared that "apocalyptic . . . was the mother of all Christian theology." He denied that Jesus taught within the apocalyptic, end-time framework, or that he even accepted such a frame of mind. Rather, he said that Jesus preached the establishment of the reign (= kingdom) of God on earth and the immanence of God to all creation. It was only after the death and resurrection of Jesus that his followers turned to enthusiastic expectation of a speedy return of the Risen Lord, who would bring about the final victory. When the early Christians began to experience persecution and suffering, their end-time expectations grew stronger and gradually colored their recollections of the teaching of Jesus. It is in this sense that Käsemann believed apocalyptic rather than the actual preaching and teaching of Jesus to be the source of Christian tradition.

The essay of Käsemann understandably sent ripples through the scholarly community, prompting responses from two other theologians: Gerhard Ebeling and Ernst Fuchs. In substance they claimed that Jesus did indeed teach and preach out of an apocalyptic frame of mind and the gospel records authentically reflect his teaching and not simply a version substantially nuanced by his followers and biographers so as to take on apocalyptic hues. Käsemann in his turn responded to these essays and thus did a new interest in apocalyptic research emerge in the 1960's. For the present, it is safe to assume that the late Norman Perrin, New Testament scholar from the University of Chicago Divinity School, represented the majority opinion among biblical scholars when, in an address he delivered at the annual meeting of the Society of Biblical Literature in 1972, he asserted: "Modern research into the historical message of Jesus may confidently be said to have established the fact that the message featured the use of apocalyptic forms and language and wisdom forms and language. Jesus proclaimed the Kingdom of God, and the Kingdom of God is an apocalyptic symbol."

The import of this aspect of biblical research for understanding Revelation may require a little more explanation. As noted above, Revelation makes no reference at all to the earthly Jesus, or to his teaching, or preaching. It is concerned only with the glorified Jesus, particularly his redemptive death (as e.g., in 1:5; 7:14; 12:44) and especially his victorious exultation (as e.g., in 3:21; 5:5; and 17:14). This phenomenon would seem to confirm Käsemann's hypothesis that apocalyptic was developed by the followers of Jesus and did not stem from Jesus himself. Further, the cry for vengeance in 6:10 and 19:17-21, as well as the expectation of an earthly millenium in 20:2, definitely contrast with the gospel teachings of Jesus as well as the other New Testament writings.

Yet scholarly research on the Gospels and other New Testament writings during the last two decades and more strongly support Dr. Perrin's statement quoted above. Jesus did indeed use apocalyptic forms and language, even if, as Perrin claims, he used them in a different way. Thus the Book of Revelation has grown from its inherited tradition, but has also been affected by its environment in an interaction so complicated that it has yet to be completely unravelled.

Qumrân and the New Testament Environment

The New Testament testifies to the fact that the Christian community did expect the end to come soon (Cf. Mt 10:23; Mk 9:1; 1 Cor 15:51; 1 Thess 4:17). In fact the expectation was so strong and enthusiastic that it needed to be restrained (Cf. 2

Thess 2; Mk 13:5-6; and 13:21-23). Nonetheless, when circumstances of life were experienced as unduly oppressive, the apocalyptic frame of mind grew stronger and more widespread and expressed itself in a variety of writings.

The discovery of the Dead Sea Scrolls in the caves around Qumrân in 1947 added much to our knowledge of the New Testament environment. Here, just seven miles south of Jericho and fifteen miles east of Jerusalem and Bethlehem, lived a group of people whose existence and library shed new light on the apocalyptic period. Though originally the site of a fortress dating from the 8th-7th centuries BC, the archeological excavations of the ruins give evidence that Qumrân was inhabited between 131 BC to 31 BC, when it was apparently destroyed by fire and earthquake, and was again inhabited from about 1 AD to 68 AD, when it was captured and destroyed by the Roman armies.

The Qumrân sect seems to have been related to the Hasidean branch of Maccabean revolt against Antiochus Epiphanes in 167 BC (Cf. 1 Mac 2:42). The Hasideans (*Hasidim* = pious ones) supported the Zadokite priesthood as legitimate. When in 172 BC, Jason the Zadokite was replaced by a non-Zadokite, the Hasideans cast their lot with the Maccabees. With the passage of time, however, the Maccabeans became more interested in establishing a dynasty than in religious reform, and the Hasideans did not find them to be the champions they had desired.

It seems then that a Righteous Teacher, or

Teacher of Righteousness, arose in their midst to guide them "in the way of his heart." The Righteous Teacher was a priest of the Zadokite line who though persecuted by the ruling high priests survived them until he decided to take his followers to settle in Qumrân, probably around 140-130 BC. The Teacher appears to have died a natural death, and evidence indicates that another influx of inhabitants arrived around 110 BC. This group may well have been Pharisees who came to join the community because of persecution. At any rate, the community flourished until destroyed by fire and earthquake around 31 BC.

After remaining in ruins for about 30 or 40 years, the settlement was rebuilt at the beginning of the Christian era, though it is not clear what prompted such a move. What is clearly evident in the writings from this period, though, is that they were decidedly anti-Roman. This settlement was destroyed by the Roman Tenth Legion in 68 AD. Very likely some short time before the end, the community hid its manuscripts in the nearby caves.

About one fourth of the literature discovered in the caves is biblical. For instance, eight manuscripts of the Book of Daniel have been found. This surely played some role in shaping the community's expectations. In fact, we learn much from the remainder of the materials which are the writings of the inhabitants themselves. In the second period of occupation, the inhabitants of Qumrân considered themselves to be an apocalyptic community, awaiting the end-time. They expected a prophet like

Moses or Elijah whose coming would signal imminent salvation. In addition, they appeared to be
awaiting at least two messiahs: a messiah of Aaron
who would be annointed as rightful high priest, and
a messiah of Israel, who would be annointed
Davidic king.

One very significant kind of literature discovered at Qumrân is the *pesher*, or commentary on
scripture. These commentaries view biblical materials as if intended specifically and chiefly for the
Qumrân community, and not primarily for the lifetime of the biblical author. Thus the observations
made on the "righteous" by Habakkuk around 600
BC are interpreted in the Qumrân *pesher* as referring to the Teacher of Righteousness who is opposed
by the Man of the Lie who also opposes the entire
community. Certain people follow the Man of the
Lie, paying no heed to the Teacher's interpretations
of scripture. The frame of mind behind such a commentary is clearly apocalpytic, or end-time, and
probably stems from the Teacher himself.

It has been suggested that the particular cluster
of ideas just discussed is similar to the ideas in Revelation 13:5 describing the Beast (=persecutor of
the community) and 14:5 describing the faithful on
whose lips "no deceit has been found." Whether
one agrees with the suggested correspondence or
not, the fact nevertheless remains that the literature
of Qumrân sheds impressive light on the environment of the early Christians by demonstrating the
extent to which the apocalyptic frame of mind prevailed, as well as the perspective taken in interpret-

ing biblical literature as relevant to the present. The discoveries and subsequent study of the Dead Sea Scrolls served in no small way as a stimulus to renewed interest and research on apocalyptic as well as on the Book of Revelation. Josephine Ford's Anchor Bible Commentary on Revelation draws very heavily upon the Qumrân materials, providing fascinating, if sometimes debatable, insights.

The Book of Revelation

From 1973 to 1976 a Task Force on Apocalyptic Tradition met for four days of discussion at the annual meeting of the Catholic Biblical Association of America. The Task Force members each studied individual books or specific themes and shared their written research reports prior to each meeting, so that the discussion could focus on materials familiar to all the participants. Individual members have published their studies, and the entire July 1977 issue of the *Catholic Biblical Quarterly* was devoted to the topic of apocalyptic, printing articles by six of the eleven members of the group. Two of the members in particular are recognized as experts on the Book of Revelation, and their studies and surveys can facilitate a grasp of what scholars are saying today—and as a matter of fact have been saying for some time!—about the last book in the Bible.

Adela Yarbro Collins of Chicago's McCormick Theological Seminary has observed:

Perhaps the hardest won and most dearly held result of historical critical scholarship on the Revelation to John is the theory that the work must be interpreted in terms of the historical context in which it was composed. Such an approach refers the images of Revelation to contemporary historical events or to eschatological images current at the time.[11]

The historical context of Revelation can be deduced from the book itself. To begin with, it has already been noted that the author identifies himself by name: John (1:1, 4,9; 22:8), and he is apparently someone known to the community. He has been banished to the island of Patmos and thus shares in the fate of the persecuted communities to which he writes (1:10). To further identify John, it has often been asked whether he was related to John the Apostle, and whether he is also the author of the Johannine gospel and epistles. The answers to these questions are not simple. Until the 16th century, tradition generally held that John the Apostle was the author of the literature. But then various questions were raised, particularly on the basis of internal evidence: i.e., a marked difference in style between the writings raising strong doubt that one individual could be responsible for all of them. Scholars have not been able to reach a unanimous conclusion, but generally hold that the Apostle John was a great authority in Asia until the end of the 1st century. He probably inspired all the writings published under his name, but the writing and/or editing would probably have been carried out by different disciples, more or less familiar with his thought. Thus, the individual "John" responsible for composing/writing the Book of Revelation, is probably not the same "John" who composed/wrote the Gospel.

Taking into consideration the churches in the province of Asia to whom the book is addressed, scholars have been able to determine the probable time of composition, based on the contents. It is known from history that worship of the Roman emperor as a deity was promoted with special zeal in the province of Asia. This would suggest a variety of dates, depending on how one identified the given emperor: Claudius (41-54); Nero (54-68); Vespasian (69-79); Domitian (81-96); or even Trajan (98-117). But the picture of the circumstances which Revelation sketches (e.g., 13:4; 13:12; 14:9,11; 16:2; 19:20) corresponds with no epoch of early Christianity so well as with the period of Domitian's persecution.

In addition, knowledge about the seven churches also suggests this later date. Ephesus, Sardis and Laodicea have lost their first fervor; Laodicea boasts of her wealth (3:17), though she had been completely destroyed by an earthquake in 60-61 AD. Thus the date of composition, or final editing, generally accepted by the majority of scholars is about 90 to 96 AD, toward the end of the reign of Emperor Domitian.

Given these historical circumstances for the origin of the Book of Revelation, it is easy to recognize its chief purpose as offering encouragement, consolation and comfort to a church on the point of becoming a martyr church. Its advice is to stand firm in the faith and not to compromise beliefs or practices at all: soon God's promises will be fulfilled and final deliverance and vindication will favor those who remain faithful.

These basic historical data present the context in which the Book of Revelation arose and represent the "hardest won and most dearly held result of historical critical scholarship" as noted by Collins. From this perspective it is now possible to proceed to a consideration of the form of Revelation.

Revelation: A Prophetic-Apocalyptic Letter

A second member of the Task Force, Elisabeth Schuessler Fiorenza of the University of Notre Dame, has been researching and publishing her results about the Book of Revelation for more than ten years.[12] While other scholars have noted that the book manifests apocalyptic, prophetic, and to a small extent, epistolary characteristics, they have drawn no significant conclusions. Fiorenza, however, believes that it is no accident that Revelation *as a whole* has the form of the early Christian apostolic letter similar to those written by Paul. It is also no accident, she believes, that the prophetic-apocalyptic visions, symbols, and patterns are set within an epistolary framework. The overall form of Revelation appears therefore to mark it as a Christian prophetic-apocalyptic circular letter, or more precisely a prophetic-apocalyptic book playing the role of an apostolic open letter, a public pastoral if you will, to seven (i.e., all the) churches in Asia Minor.

Let us consider this framework of Revelation. After a superscription (1:1-3) which is very much like Amos 1:1-2, there is a passage similar to the opening of a Pauline letter: 1:4-6. We read a salutation (1:4a) identifying the recipients as the churches of Asia, and the sender as John; a blessing (1:4b-5a): "grace and peace, etc."; and a doxology (1:5b-6): "To him be glory, etc." The concluding greeting in Revelation 22:21: "The grace of the Lord Jesus be with you all. Amen" is also similar to the conclusions of Pauline letters. Moreover, these beginning and end segments in Revelation form what is known as an "inclusion," i.e., a literary device of repeating words or phrases, signifying the author's intention of marking off a unit.

In addition to this obvious epistolary frame in the Book of Revelation, the first segment of the book records seven letters to seven churches. From the point of view of content, John Dominic Crossan of DePaul University has noted that the structure of these seven letters is similar to the second and third letters attributed to John:[13]

- opening address;
- praise, mentioning good points, or warning, mentioning bad points;
- judgment, speaking both threats and rewards;

- promise of a future visit;
- final greetings.

Thus here in Revelation there is the name of the church receiving the letter; some aspect of Christ repeated from the initial vision; praise for good points, warning against bad points; threats and rewards as judgment is passed; and conclusions.

Fiorenza refines these observations by identifying five sections in each letter on the basis of literary indicators:

1. an address and commission to write;
2. a prophetic messenger formula (a Greek phrase that can be translated "has this to say," reminiscent of the classical prophetic "Thus says the Lord!") presented with a characteristic of Christ drawn from the inaugural vision as the subject of the formula;
3. the phrase, "I know" followed by a description of a situation, a censure, a call to repentance; the word "see" followed by a revelatory statement; or an announcement of the Lord's coming. This segment ends with an exhortation.
4. A call to hear the message directed to all: "Let him who has ears . . .";
5. An end-time promise phrased in Greek with the participial form of the word translated as "victor," followed by a verb in the future tense.

Fiorenza's description of the letter-outline demonstrates the kind of scholarship urged by the Second
Vatican Council, scholarship based on the canons
of sound literary approaches.

The literary form of these letters, so nearly
identical, tells the reader that they probably never
had an independent existence, but were most likely
written expressly for the Book of Revelation. The
hortatory conclusion ("Let him who has ears . . .")
of the letters is clearly trying to individualize or
personalize the message. In general, though, the letters seem to suggest that the greatest threat lies not
so much in oppression from without, as from
heterodoxy or falling from faith, within.

The specific content of the letters sheds very
important light on the situations of the churches and
helps understand the overall situation which Revelation addresses. But an intelligent reading of the
letters requires some background information about
the communities which may have been very obvious to the initial recipients and readers of the book,
but are not so obvious to contemporary readers. If,
as Prof. Collins advises, one must refer the images
of Revelation to contemporary historical events, it
is impossible to read the book without reference to
other information about the churches.

Ephesus (2:1-7) was a cultural and religious
center, the seat of the proconsular government,
though not the capital, and a commercial metropolis
in Asia due to the many trade routes that extended
between Greece and Asia Minor by way of the
Cayster River. (Obviously, unless the modern

reader is world-travelled, a map is indispensable for proper reading of this section of Revelation.) The church at Ephesus was founded by Paul around 53-56, though a riot was also fomented against him in the great theater (Acts 19:34). Its temple to Artemis was one of the seven wonders of the world, and it was also associated with emperor worship. While the letter praises the church members, it does mention that they have fallen from previous heights and that their earlier fervor has cooled. Though the letter is no more specific than this, an educated guess at the problems in Ephesus might be based on Acts 20:17-38, Eph 4:17-32, and 5:10-20. If indeed the Ephesians have yielded to the suggested temptations, the encouragement to reform and repent becomes intelligible.

Smyrna (2:8-11) was the most important city of Asia after Ephesus with whom (as well as with Pergamum) it often vied for prestige. After the destruction of Jerusalem in 70 AD, Smyrna became a favorite settlement for Jews, and they became powerful in the city and particularly hostile to the Christian community there. The Smyrnian Christians are encouraged to remain faithful, even to death if necessary, for the testing period will be brief but the reward will last forever.

Pergamum (2:12-17) was famous for its religious monuments, especially the one in honor of Asclepius, patron of healing. It was the center for emperor worship in Asia. The letter appears to chastise the Christian inhabitants for succumbing to libertinism (eating meat offered to idols, and "fornication," or idolatry—emperor worship) and urges reform. The statement, "I come soon" (2:16) makes its first appearance here and occurs a total of seven times in Revelation (3:11; 16:15; 22:2,12,17,20), underscoring the theme that the glorious Christ will intervene in human history and real politics very soon in order to save as well as to judge.

The city, Thyatira (2:18-29), was of far less importance than the preceding cities, and its situation gave it an appearance of dependence (upon Pergamum) and subjection, as well as weakness. But its military significance—it could harbor soldiers to protect the road between Pergamum and Sardis—gave it some measure of importance. First century coins attest to the presence of weaving, leather, pottery and bronze melting industries in this city. The significance of this information is that each industry had its own special trade guild, whose members would be expected to pay homage to the emperor as a deity in order to prove their worker-loyalty to him. Obviously, such circumstances heightened the likelihood of syncretism.

Be that as it may, the letter to Thyatira suggests that the danger for the city is internal, due to the effect of a prophetess leading the people astray in the manner of a Jezebel (cf. 1 Kg 21:21-24). Perhaps this woman condoned the consequences of labor-guild proofs of loyalty (idolatry and eating meats sacrificed to idols). Punishment for this will be severe, so repentance is urged. The salvation promised seems particularly fitting given the second-rate posture of the city: it will ultimately have great dominion over nations (2:27).

The residents of Sardis (3:1-6) had a reputation in their time for luxurious and licentious living. Its predominant worship was the orgiastic cult of Cybelle, nature goddess of Anatolia. It is difficult to determine the specific problem in Sardis. Being alive but really dead probably indicates that in spite of every evidence of life, true spiritual existence has died out! In fact, the letter has no praise for Sardis at all. It is nonetheless encouraged to reform, lest it be overtaken quite unexpectedly with disaster before it has an opportunity to repent.

Philadelphia (3:7-13), too, held an important place on the imperial post road of the first century as an entrance further east. It was frequently destroyed by earthquakes, so its population was small, and perhaps "weak" too. At one time it was designated "Temple Warden," and so it was definitely involved in emperor worship, but for some unknown reason the inhabitants had won a promise of divine protection in the imminent destruction. This modicum of fidelity was judged sufficient to merit deliverance and salvation, but it did not obviate encouragement to continue in fidelity.

Finally, Laodicea (3:14-22) was an important agricultural and marketing center, as well as a banking center and a large manufacturing center of clothing and carpets of native grown black wool. In addition, this city was the seat of a flourishing medical school from which came a well-known eye salve (phrygian powdered stone, like mascara now used to paint the eyes). This city's prosperity was great and it grew quite self-sufficient, so that when destroyed by earthquakes in 60-100 AD, she was able to refuse imperial subsidies and could afford to rebuild herself.

Perhaps such self-sufficiency led to tepidity, and a self-satisfied feeling in spiritual matters. This could have been abetted by an apparent lack of outstanding evil, or any persecution in the community. The letter warns that true riches and satisfaction are spiritual and come from a spiritual rather than a material source. Only through timely repentance will the inhabitants deserve to participate in the end-time banquet.

Taken together, the letters present a very real, even if somewhat stylized, description of the communities in Asia. The praise-worthy characteristics of these communities stand out as mutual love and service to others, fidelity and endurance, adherence to what has been taught, and rejection of all false prophecy and teaching. But clearly not all the communities deserved praise. Some were more dead than alive, others had slipped from previous levels of enthusiasm, love, zeal, ardor, and still others flirted dangerously with erroneous teachings and appeared willing to practice or believe anything, so long as it was pragmatically useful.

There is no doubt that the overall message is a repeated summons to repentance, to reformation, or to steadfastness in the faith. The communities addressed in these letters are vexed by persecutions from Jews in their midst, deceptions from errant

Christian teachers, and the ever increasing demands for emperor worship in the context of the ever-spreading Roman civil religion. Of course, in the letters the apocalyptic frame of mind emerges when Satan is deemed to be behind all these difficulties. Nevertheless, a promise of victory is given to all who persevere through to the end-time.

As the average Bible-reader realizes, the above description of the situations of the churches mentioned in Revelation is not readily evident from the biblical text itself. This explains why many readers often chose to make spiritual applications from this material in preference to struggling to learn the historical context of the discussions. The foregoing descriptions have been based on commentaries such as Ford's. While espousing a debatable general hypothesis in her commentary, she has nevertheless compiled a wealth of illustrative materials from archeology, history, and a wide array of biblically-related literature, including the Dead Sea Scrolls. She has also included clear illustrations redrawn from various photographs of pertinent artifacts. This is the only reasonable way in which one can possibly hope to arrive at an understanding of Revelation within the context of its times. Interestingly enough, the popular and inexpensive (then 30 cents) commentary on the Book of Apocalypse in the New Testament Reading Guide published by Liturgical Press, Collegeville, MN., already in 1962 had presented such an approach for the average reader, though obviously on a much smaller scale.

Summary

    While waxing and waning over the course of time, biblical scholarship on Revelation received new stimulus in recent decades from renewed interest in the role apocalyptic played in the life and teachings of Jesus, as well as from the increased understanding of apocalyptic drawn from research on Qumrân, its literature, and especially its interpretations of scripture.

    Contemporary scholarship on Revelation basically takes a literary and historical approach. Historically, the book is a product of its time: namely, the persecution of Christians in Asia Minor by the Roman Emperor Dominian, who like his predecessors, demanded worship of himself as a deity. This took place toward the close of the first century of the common era—a century noted as apocalyptic in outlook in the Jewish and Christian milieus. Revelation can only be understood against this backdrop.

    From the literary perspective, Revelation manifests three sets of characteristics: those common to apocalyptic literature, reviewed in chapter one; those common to epistles, reviewed in this chapter; and those peculiar to prophecy, to be taken up in the next chapter.

3
The Prophetic Character and Message of Revelation

Though scholars have long known the epistolary "super-structure" of Revelation, they have tended to minimize its significance because of the other obvious dimensions of the book: the prophetic-apocalyptic. Even Fiorenza, who appears to give the epistolary characteristics more attention and prominence than other scholars, points to the fact that Revelation as a letter doesn't read like a letter.

Indeed, a second look at the beginning and end of Revelation shows that in addition to epistolary characteristics, it also bears the marks of a book of prophecy. At the very outset John asserts: "Happy is the man who reads this prophetic message . . ." (1:3) The conclusion of that verse is noteworthy, since it qualifies the prophetic message exactly as it was understood in the tradition of Jewish scriptures: "for the appointed time is near," and all this "must happen very soon." John's message — like the prophecy of antiquity — was an announcement of God's plans and will for the here and now, and not for distant centuries or epochs.

Similarly, Revelation concludes with this observation: "I myself give witness to all who hear the prophetic words of this book," and it adds the curse patterned after Deuteronomy 4:3 ("In your observance of the commandments of the Lord, your God, which I enjoin upon you, you shall not add to what I command you nor subtract from it"): "If anyone adds to these words, God will visit him with all the plagues described herein! If anyone takes from the words of this prophetic book, God will take away his share in the tree of life and the holy city described here" (Rev 22:18-19).

In literary criticism, the correspondence just identified (1:3 and 22:18-19) is known as an inclusion, a literary device employed by authors to mark the limits of units. Enclosing the entire Book of Revelation as these verses do, it seems as if the author definitely intended his book also to be known as prophecy. He calls it such in other sections of the book (cf. 19:10; 22:7, 10). He clearly aligns himself with the great prophetic tradition of Judaism.

It is for this reason that Fiorenza, echoing other scholars, identifies Revelation as prophetic-apocalyptic. Such a hyphenated description makes good sense, for, as Hanson has pointed out, apocalyptic developed out of prophecy. In Revelation, the message takes on an apocalyptic dimension and bears apocalyptic literary traces, but it is essentially a prophetic message couched in prophetic forms, even while calling upon apocalyptic imagery. We shall examine some of the prophetic forms and then focus on the prophetic message of Revelation.

Prophetic Forms in Revelation

The classical prophets of antiquity invariably reported what came in later centuries to be identified as an inaugural or commissioning vision. Isaiah (6:1ff) and Jeremiah (1:1ff), for instance, report a dialogue with God in which each is made privy to his plans for Israel and is then sent to announce these plans to the people. In Rev 1:9-20 John describes what appears to be intended by him as his inaugural or commissioning vision. Having been exiled for professing his faith, he has a vision and is instructed to write down . . . and—in contrast with apocalyptic writers who are generally instructed to seal the message up for a period of time—to publish it among his fellow-believers. Analogous commissioning visions are repeated in Revelation 4-5 and 10:1-11:2, both marking off sections of new materials.

The vision in Revelation 4-5 appears at the end of the seven letters, and introduces the second and third septets: viz., discussion of the seven seals and the seven trumpets. Revelation 4-5 bear a striking resemblance to Ezekiel's inaugural vision (1:5-20). The vision of the seals reports familiar characteristics of the end-time expected by Christians: appearance of an anti-Christ figure, war, hunger, and death, very similar to the outlook recorded in Mark

13. But the vision of the trumpets (and later the bowls) portrays the end-time as a period of cosmic catastrophes with plagues strikingly reminiscent of the Exodus experience so as to suggest that God's day of wrath will really be like an exodus for his new people from the bondage of anti-God forces.

The vision in Revelation 10:1—11:2 introduces the explanation of the content of the little scroll which is unfolded in chapters 12 to 14. This scroll, explicitly characterized as prophetic interpretation of the Christian community's situation, will be discussed in the second section of this chapter.

Prophets of old spoke their messages in forms which have now come to be known as prophetic judgment speeches. Essentially, their speeches featured two parts: an indictment and an announcement of judgment (hence the title). To assure the listener that this was not simply a prophet's whim but the actual will of God, the prophet repeated the phrase: "Thus says the Lord." This signalled the prophet to be God's messenger. Thus, the opening chapters of the book of the Prophet Amos illustrate a very simple form of this pattern: "Thus says the Lord, because of such crimes, I will render such punishment, says the Lord."

In Revelation, the letters to the churches are good illustrations of this judgment speech pattern. The phrase "the words" or "has this to say" is equivalent to "Thus says the Lord." Then follows a message (censure, praise, encouragement) and a judgment for failure to repent, or a promise of future reward for those who persevere in fidelity.

Again, prophets of old sometimes acted out their message in what has been identified as prophetic symbolic actions. The report of these actions in scripture involves three elements: a command sending the prophet; the execution of the action directed by God; and the explanation by the prophet of the significance of the action, using the phrase: "Thus says the Lord." An example of this can be seen in Ezekiel 3:1-3: "He said to me: Son of man, eat what is before you; eat this scroll, then go, speak to the house of Israel. So I opened my mouth and he gave me the scroll to eat. Son of man, he then said to me, feed your belly and fill your stomach with this scroll I am giving you. I ate it, and it was sweet as honey in my mouth. He said: Son of man, go now to the house of Israel and speak my words to them."

In Revelation 10:8-11 John reports a similar experience: "Then the voice which I heard from heaven spoke to me again and said, 'Go, take the open scroll from the hand of the angel standing on the sea and on the land.' I went up to the angel and said to him, 'Give me the little scroll,' He said to me, 'Here, take it and eat it! It will be sour in your stomach, but in your mouth it will be sweet as honey.' I took the little scroll from the angel's hand and ate it. In my mouth it tasted as sweet as honey, but when I swallowed it my stomach turned sour. Then someone said to me, 'You must prophesy again for many peoples and nations, languages and kings.' " The similarity to Ezekiel is unmistakable. It is obvious that John places himself squarely in the prophetic tradition.

Other prophetic forms abound in Revelation: there are vision reports, oracles, woe oracles, announcements of judgment, proclamations of salvation, prophetic commands, and many others. Yet often a certain apocalyptic coloring is given to the forms.

Consider the literary form of macarisms (so called from the Greek, *makarismos*, translating the Hebrew *'ašrê*, and rendered in English as "blessed"—whence the beatitudes—or "happy"). The macarism is essentially a poetic saying that intends to convey a culturally valuable attitude or manner of conduct. It was used in Jewish wisdom literature (e.g., "Happy the man who finds wisdom, the man who gains understanding," Prov 3:13; also Ps 1:1; Prov 8:32; etc.) to describe a value in the here-and-now conducive to present well-being. It was also used in Jewish apocalyptic circles (e.g., "Blessed is he who waits and comes to the thousand three-hundred and thirty-five days," Dan 12:12; cf. also Tob 13:14, and the extra-biblical literature like Henoch, etc.) to describe a value in the here-and-now conducive to future well-being. The apocalyptic macarisms often had a motive clause or phrase appended, since it was not always obvious why such a line of conduct for the here-and-now was praiseworthy.

There is an interesting assortment of seven macarisms in the Book of Revelation: 1:3; 14:13; 16:15; 19:9; 20:6; 22:7,14. Revelation 1:3 and 22:7 are nearly identical: "Happy is the man who reads this prophetic message, and happy are those who hear it and heed what is written in it, for the appointed time is near"; and "Remember, I am coming soon. Happy the man who heeds the prophetic message of this book." Both instances illustrate the apocalyptic form of macarism (because they add the motive: the end-time is near!) though they center on a prophetic message. This is but one small indication of how the author uses apocalyptic imagery and figures to express his prophetic message and to serve the purpose of prophetic admonition and interpretation.

Scholars have not identified any literary form as an apocalyptic literary form. All they have been able to do is list characteristics peculiar to the literature. In Revelation, the symbolism and mythical images, the coded language and symbolic numbers, the literary devices of visions and auditions, the cosmological stage-setting and the end-time expectation and hope for the future clearly mark the book as an apocalyptic book. Nevertheless, other key elements peculiar to apocalyptic such as pseudonymity, secrecy, division of history into definite pre-determined periods, journeys through the heavenly world in order to learn the message, or extensive lists of revealed things are conspicuously absent. Fiorenza seems correct then in describing Revelation as a prophetic-apocalyptic book.

Throughout the entire book, John used dramatic, liturgical, mythopoeic, and Christian language and patterns, in addition to the apocalyptic and prophetic formats, to formulate his own literary account of early Christian prophecy. Yet the overall character of the book is strongly prophetic. Viewed as a whole, Revelation is shaped like a prophetic book. It begins with an exhortation and interpretation of the Christian situation in the form of a prophetic vision (1:9-3:22). The center of the book (10-14) is explicitly defined as a prophetic interpretation of the political and religious situation of the community (10-11). In fact, since this prophetic scroll is situated centrally in the book's arrangement, it seems quite clear that the main function of Revelation is the prophetic interpretation of the community's situation. Finally, the book ends with visionary promise and exhortation (19:11-22:9), just like a book of prophecy.

The Prophetic Message of Revelation

One thing that still eludes scholars is complete agreement on the outline of Revelation. The outline, or structure, is quite important in arriving at the message of the book. Various outlines have been proposed, and in general, chapters 4 to 21-22 are usually identified as the central part of the book.

Noting the patterning of sevens in the book (seven letters, seals, trumpets, and bowls) and believing that the process she calls "intercalation" (that is interrupting something like a series of seven before it ends to begin something different, after which the original item is concluded) helps explain the apparent illogicality of arrangement in the book,

Fiorenza has proposed a patterned outline of the material in this fashion:

A 1:1-8 (epistolary, prophetic, macarismic opening)
  B 1:9-3:22 (inaugural vision and seven letters - promises)
    C 4:1-9:21; 11:15-19 (second vision: seven seals and seven trumpets)
      D 10:1-15:4 (Little scroll-prophetic interpretation of present)
    C' 15:1,5-19:10 (seven bowls continuation from trumpets)
  B' 19:11-22:9 (visions of final salvation - fulfillment)
A' 22:10-22:21 (epistolary, prophetic, macarismic closing)

An outline similar to this had been proposed years ago by John Dominic Crossan for the Gospel of John, so Fiorenza's proposal is not entirely unprecedented. Other scholars may object to the outlines or segments of them, but there seems to be general agreement that the central features thus isolated are indeed the recognized central portions of the book. Fiorenza's concentric outline of Revelation singles out 10:1-15:4 as the center of the book, around which the other parts have been arranged in mutual relationship: A to A', B to B', and C to C'. It is to this central section that we now turn more concentrated attention in order to grasp what scholars identify as the prophetic message of the book.

In the text of Revelation as illustrated on the outline here (see sections C and D), the development of the seven trumpets is broken after the sixth (Rev 9:12-20), and in Revelation 10-11 there appear two commissioning visions: one similar to Ezekiel 3:1-3 (eating the scroll), and another similar to Zechariah 2:5-9 (measuring the temple). Eating the scroll signifies both good news and bad news: the good news is that final deliverance and victory are at hand; the bad news is that it will happen only after much persecution and suffering have taken place. The little scroll is open and therefore the message is understood as intended for all to know.

The command to seal up the message (10:4-5) is strange and contrary to the otherwise normal commands in Revelation to write the message down (1:11,19; 14:13; 19:9; 21:5) and to make it known to all (22:10). It has been suggested that this instruction may be an indication of the limited nature and applicability of these immediate revelations with their pertinence intended mainly to the actual persecution of Christians under Domitian toward the end of the first century.

Measuring the temple is a symbol of protection. The temple refers to the Jerusalem edifice (no longer existing) but to the Christian community which is known as the temple of God in Christian literature (1 Cor 3:16ff; 2 Cor 6:16; Eph 2:19-21; 1 Pet 2:5). The 42 months is equivalent to 1260 days or three and a half years, a number half of seven and therefore symbolizing short duration. The message of this passage is that the persecuted church is indeed protected; its persecution will not last long.

The two witnesses cannot be identified with certainty, though they are reminiscent of prophets like Moses and Elijah (Dt 18:15; Mal 3:22-14) expected, as at Qumrân, to return at the end-time. The great city/Sodom/Egypt are names which refer to Babylon (mentioned in 14:18; 16:19; 17:5,18; 18:2,10,21), the code name for Rome in this book. Again, the persecution is shown to be of short duration, and the enemy is identified. But deliverance is also announced.

The next chapters (12 to 14) introduce these figures: a woman, a dragon, a beast, and the lamb. Each figure is symbolic, representing a key agent—in code, of course—in the present situation of persecution levelled at the Asian church for resisting participation in emperor worship. The woman in Revelation 12 symbolizes the church. Her child (and the rest of her offspring in v.17) represent the members of the Church. The dragon (ancient serpent, devil or satan in v. 9) is an echo of the mythical monster infamous in the literature of antiquity and epitomizes the forces of evil opposed to God. In biblical literature analogues to the dragon are Rahab (Is 51:9; Job 26:12f; Ps 89:10) and Leviathan (e.g., Ps 74:13f).

The dragon summons the aid of a beast, in fact, two beasts. The first beast, who has the appearance of a counterfeit lamb (wounded head), does the work of the dragon. Coming as it does from the sea (viewed geographically from Asia), this beast would appear to be the Roman Empire, perhaps in the person of an emperor, who insists on worship of himself as a deity. The second beast, coming from the land, is probably from the country itself. It is presented as a false prophet (16:13; 19:20; 20:10), a counterfoil to the lamb in the religious sphere, and perhaps represents the pagan priesthood which had the task of promoting emperor worship.

The symbolic number of the beast, given in Revelation 13:18, has long exercised human ingenuity in attempts at gaining a clear identification. With evidence thus far available, a precise and unequivocal identification is impossible. The most commonly accepted interpretation, however, is that the number describes the Emperor Nero. The Hebrew language has no numerals as such, but uses letters of the alphabet as numbers. The Hebrew phrase meaning "Caesar Nero" (=nrwn qsr) tallied up to 666 in this way: 50 - 200 - 6 - 50 - 100 - 60 - 200. Intriguingly, the Latin form of the title amounts to 616, an alternative reading found in other ancient manuscripts. This is not to say that the passage necessarily refers to Nero in person during his reign. He was the first emperor to persecute the Christians. The worst characteristics attributed to this beast seem to fit Nero, and tradition believed that though he died, he became incarnate in succeeding emperors, and particularly in Domitian. This process of seeking hidden meanings in passages through numerical values is called *gematria*. It is very popular in Jewish exegesis of the Bible.

Revelation 14 portrays the final victory of the

church over this persecution through the efforts of the lamb. This figure has been introduced earlier in Revelation (5:6) and is used 28 times throughout the book as Christ's main title. The image rings echoes with the understanding of Christ sacrificed like a lamb, as in John 1:29,36; 19:36; Acts 8:32; 1 Cor 5:7; 1 Peter 1:18f, which has been inspired by two key themes in the Hebrew scriptures: the servant of the Lord (Is 53:7) and the passover lamb (Ex 12). The Book of Revelation, however, presents the lamb as a conquering victor, one who after his sacrificial death rules over the entire universe. With him are the 144,000, the "remnant" mentioned often in the Hebrew scriptures (e.g., Is 4:2-3; 10:19-21; 28:5-6; Jer 3:14; Zeph 2:7-9; Rom 11:5), who are virgins, that is, who are not idolators, who have not yielded to pressures for worshipping a false god. Idolatry in the Hebrew scriptures was often represented as harlotry, hence the notion of virginity indicates fidelity to the worship of the one true God.

The final portion of Revelation 14:6-20 offers consolation to the community by saying that judgment is about to take place. The persecuting forces will fail, lose power, and those who have persevered, indeed even to martyrdom, will receive the reward. The promise of a reward is "what sustains the holy ones, who keep the commandments of God and their faith in Jesus" (14:12). Thus, in brief, does the seer John offer prophetic here-and-now interpretation of the present political and religious situation of his fellow believers in the Asian church and thus does he encourage them to be faithful in endurance (13:9-10) so as to merit the final deliverance which is imminent.

Further detailed discussion of these chapters and their individual verses lies beyond the scope of this book, for what has been noted well represents what the majority of biblical scholars have been saying in modern times about the Book of Revelation's central message. It is on the details that variations occur, and for that, the reader is encouraged to consult more lengthy commentaries.

Options for the Community

For people in the kind of political situation in which the Asian Christians found themselves, there were a variety of options. In a similar historical context of persecution under Antiochus Epiphanes, some Jews chose to mount an active revolution. The Maccabees as described in the biblical books bearing their names pursued such a course of action. They believed so strongly in their position that they were convinced that they did not fight alone, but were accompanied by heavenly beings as well (2 Mac 2:21; 5:1-4; 10:29-31; 15:8-16).

A similar position was adopted by the Zealots who were quite active in the first two centuries of the common era. They believed in active opposition to the Roman oppressors and were responsible for fomenting the Jewish war against Rome (66-70 AD) which ended with the destruction of the temple, as well as for the second rebellion against Rome in

132-135 AD, when Rabbi Akiba publicly declared Simon Bar Kochba (=Ben Kosiba) to be the long-awaited Messiah. Simon's dismal failure quashed messianic hope in Israel for a very long period of its history.

Another option was one taken by those who disagreed with violent rebellion or revolution. While the Maccabees fought back, others preferred to join the oppressors. This group represented those who began, under Antiochus, to bid for the high priesthood, since he had declared that it would no longer be hereditary but would be given to the highest bidder. This would be equivalent to modern apocalyptic attitudes expressed in such assertions as "better red than dead," or "if you can't beat 'em, join 'em." Though the Maccabees themselves at first did not favor such a view, in the years following their victory their desire to establish a dynasty caused them to flirt with this kind of outlook.

A third option, following the suggestion of Adela Collins, might be termed passive resistance. Her distinction between purely passive and synergistic passive resistance is very helpful. A purely passive kind of resistance to persecution is simple endurance and patient waiting. To some extent the Qumrân community illustrate the purely passive type of resistance. While they supported the Maccabees in resisting oppression, they ultimately left the scene of action and retired to the desert, to their library. For all their talk of holy war, they did not seem eager to engage in active revolutionary resistance, at least not until the final decisive battle when indeed the elect would play an important role. (One scholar wryly observed that the Qumrân war scroll might have been written as choreography for a sacred ballet, since its warriors had to be 60 years old or older, and they were to enter battle encumbered with large banners proclaiming lengthy messages as well as other items.)

The Book of Daniel also appears to propose passive resistance. True, a violent battle resulting in the defeat of the persecuting powers is expected, but the elect will not participate. It will be waged by supra-human forces, while the faithful simply await the outcome. The tales in Daniel (1-6), which probably originated in situations prior to the Antiochan persecution, illustrate a passive resistance which is always followed by rescue of those involved. When Antiochan persecution broke out, it was obvious that some of the passive resisters would be killed (11:33-35). But sections of Daniel stemming from these circumstances continue to suggest a simple passive resistance even to the point of death. It certainly does not seem to favor the revolutionary activity of the Maccabees. Daniel 8:25 clearly affirms that Antiochus "will be broken without a (human) hand being raised." Rather, the faithful are urged to "remain loyal" (i.e., be faithful to the covenant and resist temptations to the contrary). "The nation's wise men shall instruct the many," and though some will fall, the rest shall be tested, "refined and purified, until the end-time" (11:32-35; 12:12).

The second type of passive resistance termed by Collins as synergistic takes into account suffering even to the point of death for the sake of the faith. Such passive resistance is considered to add something to hastening the end-time along. It is found in the Assumption of Moses, a Jewish apocalyptic work dating from 4 BC to 6 AD and reinterpreting Deuteronomy 31-34. In this work which portrays the leaders as failures, the voluntary death which Taxo and his seven sons freely accepted rather than transgress God's commands brings on the manifestation of the reign of God. The belief is that "our blood shall be avenged before the Lord."

Revelation appears to propose this kind of passive resistance. In Chapter 12, the woman and child (church and its members) are rescued, but there is no indication of self-defense or active resistance on their part. The images of Chapter 13 are, as indicated, primeval images of supra-human opposition to God. The advice given by John to the faithful in 13:9-10 is simply to passively suffer and accept one's fate. "Let him who has ears . . ." echoes the repeated refrain from the seven letters which is a direct exhortation to the reader or listener to follow the subsequent advice. That advice is to take a passive role: "If one is destined for captivity, to captivity he goes. If one is destined to be slain by the sword, by the sword will he be slain! Such is the faithful endurance that distinguishes God's holy people" (see also 12; 2:10).

As subsequent chapters in Revelation bear out, Christ and the heavenly armies defeat the beast and his cohorts (19:11-16). Satan is bound by an angel in 20:1-3, and the last resurgence of chaos in 20:7-10 is devoured by fire come down from heaven. If any synergism, i.e., accompanying activity, is left to the faithful, it is that of filling up the number of those who must die for the faith, before final deliverance can come about (cf. Rev. 6:9-11). This resembles the concept in the Assumption of Moses.

The motivation for such passive resistance to the point of death is obviously the example of Christ. In John's inaugural vision, Christ describes himself as "the . . . One who lives. Once I was dead but now I live—forever and ever. I hold the keys of death and the nether world" (1:17-18). This is repeated in Revelation 2:8ff with the exhortation: "Remain faithful until death, and I will give you the crown of life." The example of Christ who suffered, died, and was raised from the dead makes suffering and death tolerable, gives them value, and allows for the growth of hope which can transcend persecution and death. "They defeated him (the accuser) by the blood of the lamb, and by the word of their testimony; love for life did not deter them from death" (Rev 12:11; also 20:4-6a).

Summary

The researches and studies of Fiorenza and Collins as summarized and highlighted represent the majority position of biblical research today on the Book of Revelation. As Fiorenza points out, the book is a prophetic-apocalyptic treatise encapsulated in letter form to serve as a public, pastoral letter to the faithful in Asia.

The book contains many examples of basic prophetic literary forms and explicit assertions indicating that the author viewed himself as standing in the prophetic tradition and viewed his work as prophecy. True to this tradition, he intended only to explain and interpret the present political and religious situation of his fellow believers in the context of the design of God. His aim was to offer consolation and exhortation to fidelity.

Given the urgency of the times, it is not surprising to see that the author also utilized apocalyptic images and figures in formulating his prophetic message. Coded language veils the real actors: the Church, Triumphant Christ, Satan, the Roman Empire.

But the prophetic message is clear. The present distress, though severe, will be short-lived. The powers of evil will be destroyed in a final, cosmic conflict to be waged by supra-human forces. The faithful must patiently wait, endure suffering and persecution even to the point of death. This, as Collins indicates, will help hasten the final deliverance. Christ, victoriously risen, is the model for all Christians. This, in a nutshell, is what scholars have been saying is the message of the Book of Revelation.

4
Popular Understanding
of the Book of Revelation

The preceding three chapters have sketched at least in summary the highlights of what the majority of critical biblical scholarship is saying about the Book of Revelation. In a word, the book must be viewed as a writing of its time and must be interpreted within that specific historical context. Some readers may have found this a pleasant review of things already known, or an amplification of things previously learned. Other readers may have found the presentation quite new and unfamiliar and curiously lacking in commentary and explanation about the end of the world. For these readers it is apparently clear that the book lays claim to revealing "what must happen very soon" (1:1) i.e., soon within the time frame of the present reading. And the message of the book has a ring of finality about it: everything will soon come to an end, Period.

The fact that no current critical scholarship teaches this position suggests that there may be a gap between what is known by scholars and generally taught in universities and seminaries and what is known and believed by some (perhaps the average) Bible readers. This chapter will explore some reasons for this gap by first discussing the relationship of scholars to the general public, and then reviewing Revelation in the liturgy—the place where most Christians hear the Bible read and explained.

Scholarship and the General Public

If indeed there is a gap between what scholars know and teach and what the general public has learned, scholars themselves may have to accept some blame for failing to communicate. In part, this can be blamed on the scientific training undergone by critical biblical scholars. Scientific demands for completeness, accuracy, and thoroughness often discourage a scholar from popularizing because of a general feeling that such a presentation is necessarily incomplete and perhaps even deceptive without all the details. Moreover, there is also the normal socialization process undergone by all scholars whereby they become so accustomed to reading the texts in the original languages and to utilizing the scientific shorthand and precise but generally unfamiliar vocabulary (like apocalyptic or eschatological), that in a sense they forget how to speak plain English. Finally, other pressing demands on the time of scholars frequently leaves precious little time and energy for engaging in *haute-vulgarisation*.

On the other hand, the increased attention being given to modern biblical scholarship in the media by journalists and those who specialize in popularization has not always been felicitous. For every solidly researched and well written novel like James Michener's *The Source*, there are dozens which are little more than brilliant exercises in fantasy and imagination. Newspapers have attempted to report new discoveries more regularly than hitherto, and some even have regular features on biblical topics. Headlines, however, often belie or misrepresent the content and even the thrust of the articles (and this not only for biblical articles!). Perhaps if trained biblicists were hired to write such articles or at least consulted in such writing, communication of the results of research to the general public could be improved. But biblicists themselves are often curiously unresponsive to inaccurate or deceptive media presentation and once again must bear some share of the blame for popular misunderstandings of contemporary research.

This is not to say that scholars have miserably failed to instruct the general populace. As noted earlier in this booklet, The Liturgical Press of Collegeville, Minn., published a splendid commentary on the Book of Revelation in 1962. It was brief, clear, and very inexpensive. Similar commentaries appeared at that time and have continued to appear even to the present day. Why these commentaries and study aids have not been known or utilized as widely as might be desirable is unknown. The fact remains that they are reliable and available and substantially present the same notions highlighted in this present book.

These last observations turn attention to the general public. Why has it not searched out such commentaries? Why has it not generally favored the historical and literary approaches to the Book of Revelation? The answers to these questions are probably varied and complex, but some basic observations are possible.

To begin with, the Book of Revelation, if read without the aid of commentaries, maps, and other aids, is not readily or easily understood. Yet the average Bible reader is reluctant to admit that the scriptures are difficult to understand. The result is that Revelation is read primarily for its "spiritual" value, i.e., for "what it says to me now," which often means complete disassociation from the historical circumstances in which it arose and the historical situations it addressed. Beginning with the obvious statement in Revelation 1:1 that this "must happen very soon," the reader—and sometimes the teacher and preacher—proceed to decode, translate, and apply the message entirely in terms of the present. Who has not heard the listing and identification of modern villains allegedly hidden in the chapters of Revelation (e.g., Hitler, Stalin, the Arabs, etc.), or the tally of nature's ravages (storms, hurricanes, eclipses, etc.) and other signs deduced from the text, all read from the perspective of the reader and not the author? This is admittedly much easier than ferreting out the obscure and unfamiliar historical circumstances of the original persecuted community and its real and particular enemy. As Raymond Brown, the noted American biblical scholar, points out, to read the Bible with intelligent understanding requires that one's biblical education be proportionate to one's general education. For many readers, biblical education has lagged far behind general education.

Second, it would probably be fair to say that Revelation is not a book that has been used much in teaching, preaching, spiritual direction or similar contexts. Rather, it would appear generally to be consulted by readers who for one reason or another find themselves in apocalyptic-like circumstances and have already developed an apocalyptic frame of mind. Groups living both on the fringe and sometimes in the center of a culture who feel as if life is senseless, human efforts to change unwelcome life situations are ineffective, and that there is no human way out of the distress often turn to Revelation for a sense of direction, comfort, consolation, and strengthening of hope for speedy supra-human resolution of the problem. It is inevitable that such groups would begin to believe that Revelation was written specifically for their own life-situation.

Emergence and intensification of an apocalyptic frame of mind among the general public can often be linked with undesirable political situations. The recent political experience in the United States over which most citizens felt they had no control was accompanied by an extraordinary increase in films with apocalyptic themes (e.g., featuring demons, demonic possession, etc) as well as songs with end-time motifs stressing patient endurance. It is a situation like this that often inspires people to turn to Revelation for help.

Considering the milieu in which Revelation was written and the circumstances it addressed, it is not surprising that it serves as a ready reference for subsequent generations who believe that they are the real addressees of the writing. Revelation 20, for example, has served through the centuries to inspire hope that Christ would be returning at any moment to establish a thousand year reign on earth, in which the persecuted faithful would share. These are the fortunate individuals who shared in the "first resurrection." Meanwhile, Satan will be bound up and peace will endure for a thousand years. Afterward, Satan will be loosed for a short while to work havoc, the sinners will rise from the dead ("the second resurrection"), but both they and Satan will be cast into hell, while the just will be taken to eternal bliss in heaven. This outlook is known as millenarianism or chiliasm (both words referring to a thousand).

This idea is not entirely novel, since already in the Jewish apocalypses speculation is recorded concerning the length of time that would separate this age from the age to come. Calculations of the delay range from 40 to 7000 years. The book, IV Esdras, claimed it would be 1000 years, similar to the claim in Revelation. The newness of Revelation 20 lies in some of its details—still indecipherable—about the millenium.

Even soon after the book was written, a literal

interpretation of this chapter was accepted and promoted in various forms by Cerinthus, the Ebionites, the Montanists, and other heretical groups, although it was also espoused by some early Fathers of the Church like Papias, Justin the Martyr, and Tertullian. Even the great Jerome who is ordinarily intolerant of those with whom he disagrees appeared to exhibit a measure of indulgence toward the millenarianists.

In 431 AD, the Council of Ephesus condemned chiliasm (millenarianism) as a deviation from the true faith and called it a fable. With this judgment, it practically died out of the church, though over the course of centuries the notion has been revived from time to time, predictably in times of seeming futility and despair over historical situations. In the 11th century, for instance, the Abbot Joachim of Flora taught that the millenium would begin in 1260. Similar traces of such an expectation are still found among the followers of John Hus, the Anabaptists, the Mormons, the Adventists, Jehovah's Witnesses, and some modern Pentecostal movements. In 1940 a priest in South America revived and taught a mitigated form of millenarianism, but his teachings were repudiated by the Holy See in 1941.

Scholarship on this passage points to the symbolic import of the thousand year period (similar to the symbolism of all the numbers in Revelation!). As in the Jewish apocalypses, it is not intended to be pressed for literal exactness but rather proposes that a longer period of peace will follow upon the short period of suffering. Moreover, the first and second resurrections mentioned in this passage are unclear but appear to designate two aspects of the same reality: viz., the passage from death to life worked for believers in Christian baptism, and the passage from death to life at the end of one's earthly existence. The chapter has, since St. Augustine, been generally interpreted to mean that the thousand years describe the entire period of the history of the church—including all its members—from Christ's resurrection to his second coming. It is thus an indefinitely long period of time.

The chaining of Satan is a word of encouragement for the persecuted and the martyrs of John's lifetime, indicating that the presently menacing power of evil has actually been checked by the redemptive work of Christ in which all believers share. The long period of peace will come to an end in a final and furious attack of the forces of evil against the church, but they will ultimately be defeated and that will mark the end of this world and the beginning of the next.

While many puzzling details of interpretation still remain in this passage—as well as other verses in Revelation—the church clearly teaches that the text is not to be read in a fundamentalistically literal sense. The symbolic imagery and presentation in Revelation simply will not yield their message in literal interpretations.

In line of Vatican II's encouragement to scholars to pursue literary approaches, to respect the literary genre of biblical books, and to strive to interpret books of the Bible within the historical context of their origins, biblical scholars have renewed their investigations and researches into Revelation and have reached general agreement on the results sketched and highlighted in this book. The general public is encouraged to study these results and is also encouraged to continue reading Revelation for enlightenment, edification, and—when necessary—consolation. Such an approach, as well as reading done with greater frequency than only in times of apocalyptic-like duress, can do much to improve the general appreciation of the Book of Revelation. It is in fact this kind of repeated reading that is proposed for Christians in the newly revised liturgical books.

Revelation in the Liturgy

Scholars have noted that Revelation is filled with cultic symbols, liturgical actions, hymnic language, and formulas of worship. Some have even suggested that the book reflects a liturgy. While these traces are indeed present in Revelation and the reference to "hearing" the words of the book are repeated often enough to suggest a liturgy as the context of the "hearing," it should be noted that Revelation's liturgy takes place in heaven. The seer and his readers can catch a glimpse of all this through a small, open door, but there is never an invitation to participate in the heavenly liturgy or to join in singing the heavenly victory hymns. The contemporary Christian who hears these words read at earthly liturgies is encouraged to take them to heart and to find meaning in life and hope for the future in his own time on the basis of the exhortations offered by John in Revelation to the Christians of his period.

Indeed, while the practice of reading and studying the Bible outside of liturgical contexts has been revived and has grown in recent decades the main forum in which most believers heard and still hear the scriptures read and explained is the liturgy. In the Catholic liturgy prior to the Second Vatican Council, selections from the Book of Revelation were read on seven feasts during the year:

Rev 1:1-5	September 29, St. Michael the Archangel
Rev 7:2-12	November 1, All Saints
Rev 7:13-17	September 22, St. Maurice
Rev 11:19; 12:1, 10	February 11, Apparition of Mary at Lourdes
Rev 14:1-5	December 28, Holy Innocents
Rev 19:1-9	April 22, Saints Soter and Caius
Rev 19:19	May 10, Saints Gordian and Epimachus

Another reading, Revelation 5:11-14, was assigned for the Tuesday votive mass of the angels. Revelation 21:2-5 was read at the dedication of a church, and one reading which many faithful may have heard daily, though in Latin, is Revelation 14:13, the epistle of the requiem mass, in some churches the only mass celebrated nearly every day of the year.

The readings suggest that they were probably selected by dint of topical relevance to the occasion. This is why some of the selections are only one verse long! The process also reflects a practice common in the church in those days: viz., to select verses without regard for overall context and often to the neglect of reading lengthier passages. But perhaps little damage was done since on practically all but one of these occasions (November 1), the selections were read only in Latin, and unless the faithful were following the service in a missal, they did not even know that the Book of Revelation was being used.

The liturgical reforms initiated by the Second Vatican Council included a complete revision of the book of readings for the liturgy. After a preliminary two-year cycle was tested in the mid-1960's when the entire liturgy began to be celebrated in a language understandable to the laity, a freshly constructed lectionary of readings for the liturgy covering a three-year cycle was introduced in the Roman Catholic Church in 1969. Episcopalians and Presbyterians adopted it with minor modifications in 1970, the Lutherans in 1973, and subsequently other Protestant groups. Today, most Christian worshipping groups are reading or hearing read and preached the same scriptural passages week after week in their churches.

In contrast to its previous utilization in the liturgy, the Book of Revelation now receives fairly comprehensive and frequent attention. In the second year (B) of the cycle, during the weekdays of the thirty-third and thirty-fourth weeks in the year, passages selected in sequence from Revelation are read at the daily liturgy (Monday through Saturday) as the first reading. These weeks are the last weeks of the liturgical year which immediately precede Advent. The reason for this is given by the compilers of the lectionary in the introduction: "The Books of Daniel and Revelation are assigned to the end of the liturgical year since they have appropriate eschatological themes."

The fact that the book in its entirety is read during the weekdays may indeed mean that many of the faithful who do not attend daily liturgy still will not hear the book read and explained at worship. On the other hand, the laudable practice of some Christians of reading, studying and reflecting on the scriptures at home according to the three-year liturgical cycles does insure that at least once every three years the major part of Revelation will be reread.

In the third year (C) of the cycle, passages selected from the Book of Revelation are read as the second readings at the liturgies on all the Sundays after Easter (seven). Thus it is assured that at least once every three years the faithful will certainly hear readings from the Book of Revelation, since attendance at Sunday liturgies is obligatory for Catholics. The compilers of the lectionary explain the choice of these passages as seeming "most appropriate to the spirit of the Easter season, a spirit of joyful faith and confident hope."

Two comments should be made here. First, the compilers admit they made no attempt to relate all three readings at Sunday liturgies. Taking the gospel as pivotal, they attempted to match it with an appropriate first reading from the Jewish scriptures. The second reading was not intentionally selected because of its relation to either the first or third readings, but rather was selected to represent a less familiar piece of scripture to the community through sequential readings over a period of Sundays. Consequently, those attending Sunday liturgies on these days may indeed hear the scripture read, but may not necessarily hear Revelation preached or explained in the homily.

Second, the passages selected for this sequential series of readings in Cycle C are drawn from Revelation 1; 5; 7; 21; and 22. They can generally be described as "vision" reports, and in a certain sense they do indeed represent the message of Revelation. They report triumphal scenes, but also indicate that it is through suffering and faithful perseverance that the believers have merited deliverance. The readings do not enter into the distracting details of the book, and if this were all a believing Christian ever heard of Revelation, one might feel assured that s/he would have a fair grasp of the authentic sense of the book.

The new lectionary also has a third group of readings from Revelation which are presented each year: on Holy Thursday, at the mass of the blessing of the chrism celebrated at the Cathedral, Revelation 1:5-8 is read as the second reading. On the Feast of All Saints (November 1) the first reading is drawn from Revelation 7:2-4, 9-14, and is substantially the same as in the former lectionary.

It is the third reading in this group which is read annually that merits special attention. On the Feast of the Assumption of the Blessed Virgin Mary, Revelation 11:19a, 12:1-6a, 10ab is read as the first reading. This represents a slight expansion of the reading formerly assigned to the Feast of the Apparition of the Blessed Virgin Mary Immaculate at Lourdes (February 11). This composite passage is also included among the readings suggested for use in the Common of the Blessed Virgin Mary.

The history of interpretation of this passage is significant. The woman in the passage has been variously interpreted. Most of the ancient commentators have identified her with the Christian community, the church. In the middle ages, however, it was widely believed that this woman was to be understood as the Blessed Virgin Mary, mother of Jesus. Modern biblical scholars (as indicated in the previous chapter) have generally taken up the ancient interpretation with some modifications. Given this perspective, two questions immediately arise:

(1) what is the significance of what modern scholars are saying about the interpretation of Revelation 12?; and (2) have the compilers of the new lectionary selected this reading for the feasts of Mary apparently on the basis of medieval rather than on the basis of ancient or modern interpretations?

Modern Scholarship and the Woman

Modern scholars are ever interested in what the author truly intended to say. While the woman in the text may seem to be an individual, there is also a (preferred) possibility that she represents a collectivity. She is, after all, related by contrast to the harlot mentioned in Revelation 17, which symbolizes Babylon, i.e., Rome, the persecuting city. It would seem, therefore, that the woman in Revelation 12 is also a collectivity, very likely, the people of God, the true Israel of the Jewish and Christian scriptures. There is a basis for such an interpretation in the Jewish scriptures: e.g., Zion is portrayed as a woman whose husband is God (Is 54:1,5,6); who is a mother (Is 49:21); and who is in the throes of birth (Mic 4:9-10; Is 26:16; etc.). Indeed, the Jews told the story of Mother Zion who would bring forth children in Messianic times (Is 66:7-9), and as time passed the story developed into expecting within the community the birth of one person who would be deliverer, redeemer, messiah.

It should also be noted that notion is not unique to the Jewish scriptures. It is, as it were, an international myth. Fiorenza has pointed out its elements: the figure of the woman, the dragon, the child himself, his birth, and ascension. The story is found in Babylon (Damkina, Marduk, Tiamat), Egypt (Hathor/Isis, Horus, Set/Typhon), in Greece (Leto, Apollo, Python), and in Palestine (Mother Zion/Israel, Messiah, Satan/Behemoth/Leviathan). In each instance the dragon wants the unborn child in order to destroy or devour him. The yet pregnant woman is sought by the dragon because of the child she carries. The dragon is only steps away when she delivers, and the male-child is immediately snatched up to the heavens, safe from the dragon's power.

In John's lifetime, the period in which Revelation was composed, the myth was related to worship of the emperor. He was seen to be divine by assuming the role of a divine child, born of the goddess Roma, queen of heaven. What John has effectively done, so it seems, is drawn on the story conscious both of its pagan and Jewish formats, and couched his prophetic-apocalyptic message in its terms. The point of the story is that a savior-king was to appear in the ancient world. The goddess who was to bring forth the savior was pursued by a frightening monster, a personification of evil forces. Protected in a marvelous manner, the woman was able to deliver in safety and her offspring destroyed the evil monster, thereby bringing happiness and safety to the world. John appears to have borrowed details from this story, but there are distinct differences in his presentation: the child does not immediately destroy the evil monster. He is taken up to heaven where he reigns with God. John forces our attention not on the child, but upon the woman who is still exposed to the dragon's hatred.

Examining the contextual details of Revelation 12 suggests that they are ill-suited to identifying the woman as Mary. The word describing the pains of childbirth (v. 2) is used nowhere else with such a meaning, but does describe the kinds of anguish and suffering believed to accompany the coming to birth of the messianic era (Is 26:17; Is 66:7-14). Nothing in the life of Mary indicates that she was the object of persecution, driven into the desert after the birth of her child (though imaginative interpretation would probably point to the flight to Egypt). Finally, Mary was not persecuted through her other children (v. 17). The child, in John, is clearly Christ-Jesus, but the woman is more likely the community of believers from which he originated.

This is the position of modern scholarship, and interestingly enough it is the explanation offered to those who consult the superb *Guide to the Christian Assembly* written by Thierry Maertens and Jean Frisque as they prepare for participating in the liturgy with intelligent appreciation of the assigned readings. The answer to the first question then is clearly that in accord with the directives urged already by Pope Pius XII, the preacher must pay utmost attention to the literal meaning of the text as intended by the biblical author to the extent that this can be learned.

Liturgy and the Woman

The compilers of the new series of reading have left no comment explaining why they have retained this traditional reading for the feasts of Mary. Judging from the other selections from Revelation and the explanations offered, one should conclude that the compilers trust that preachers will handle Revelation 12 with the same kind of responsibility. On the other hand, considering that of all the readings in the liturgy drawn from Revelation, this one alone stands the greatest chance of being preached with regularity, one might wonder why the compilers have left preachers an opportunity to yield to the temptation of maintaining the medieval interpretations in homilies. Perhaps they trust that preachers will diligently prepare and integrate the insights of modern scholarship with past traditions.

The *Guide to the Christian Assembly* facilitates this kind of integrations with its appropriate comment following the presentation of the literal sense of Revelation 12:

> The association of this text with the Virgin Mary is traditional. Both Saint Augustine and Saint Bernard saw the woman of Revelation as a symbol for Mary, though this was foreign to the purpose of the author. All scriptural texts indeed referring to the mystery of the Church can be applied to the Virgin Mary, in that she is intimately associated with, and clarifies, the mystery of the Church, as the Second Vatican Council reminds us.[14]

The replacement of the former reading on the Feast of the Assumption (Jud 13:22-25; 15:10) with its reference to the heroine, Judith, decapitating the enemy, with this reading from Revelation 12 is an improvement. It is also an act of faith in preachers that they will deal with the text appropriately. If there has been a gap between scholarly knowledge about Revelation and what the average person knows about the book due to faulty preaching or failure to preach on the relevant texts, the revised lectionary has done much to bridge it.

Summary

While some readers of Revelation have been well aware of the interpretations of modern scholars, others— perhaps a greater number—may not have been so well informed. Popularity of such books as Hal Lindsey's *The Late, Great Planet Earth*, which provide detailed interpretations of prophecies applied to contemporary personages and events, leads one to believe that many readers of Revelation adopt a similar perspective. They read the book as a description of present-day events.

To some degree biblical scholars have failed to make the proper interpretations of Revelation well enough known. But on the other hand, the excellent popular materials that have been prepared have generally been overlooked in favor of modern-day applications of ancient prophecies. This preference may be due at least in part to its greater ease in comparison with historical and literary study, but also to a periodically intensified apocalyptic frame of mind among the general public or to segments of it. The Book of Revelation does have a message for contemporary believers, but its message is simply an encouragement to perseverance, steadfastness in faith, and strengthening of hope. To force the symbolism of Revelation to yield literal details for the present is to misunderstand the purpose of the book.

The liturgy, particularly in its revised arrangement of biblical readings spread over a three-year cycle, has carefully presented truly representative portions of Revelation for appropriate occasions in the year: Easter, the end of the church year, and special feasts. Sound homiletic aids—including the introduction to the lectionary—provide the correct focus for preachers.

Thus, both study guides and preacher's aids relative to the Book of Revelation mirror the general agreements of scholars that the book is to be interpreted with the context of its composition. Its appropriate relevance for the contemporary reader depends very much on the understanding of the book in terms of the historical period of its origins. Considering the abundance and variety of available aids, the Book of Revelation should gain increased appreciation in the years to come.

Conclusion

Faithful to the purpose of the *What Are They Saying About . . . ?* series, this book has presented the general consensus of modern biblical scholarship on the Book of Revelation. Such scholarship identifies it as a book of its time, reflecting the historical context of its origins as well as the literary forms then popular. This critical, literary-historical approach has been a growing tradition during the last century and more, and it has been approved and encouraged within the church even before the Second Vatican Council.

The general consensus of scholarship is that Revelation was authored by John and directed to the church in Asia which was suffering persecution toward the end of the first century for its steadfast refusal to worship the Emperor Domitian as a god. The message of the book is encouragement to persevere and a strengthening of hope by affirming that the present hardships will be of short duration and will ultimately result in deliverance and final victory for those who remain faithful. The literary formats used are varied, but the epistolary, apocalyptic, and prophetic are most striking. This basic interpretation has been commonly known and accepted by scholars for a long while even as they differ on the details of interpretation.

The relevance of Revelation for the contemporary Christian is that it serves also as a work of hope. Still, no critical scholar has ever applied the book in detail to contemporary political situations, nor has critical scholarship ever taught that the book describes the end of the world. This is simply an erroneous understanding of the book and a distortion of its symbolism.

Because the major effort in this book was to present the consensus of biblical scholarship, little critical evaluation of each scholar has been given. Much of the criticism would focus on details which have been omitted because their number and variety are still in many instances of unproven status. The positions here presented reflect general consensus. There are indeed other positions, but they have not been mentioned because they are less widely accepted. In the final analysis the reader must realize that in many areas of scripture including Revelation, scholars have not yet reached unanimous agreement. Nevertheless, while admitting this variety of opinion, some opinions are entirely unacceptable: e.g., the direct application of biblical prophecies to contemporary political situations, or the literal interpretation of symbols.

One final observation. Biblical scholars in general are not nearly as well known as are theologians. Women biblical scholars whose number is considerable and growing are even less well known. Therefore, in gratitude for my personal growth as a scholar due to dialogue with women classmates and colleagues, and as a contribution to the promotion of equality as all biblical scholars become better known, the researches of women have by preference been cited in this book whenever possible.

Notes

1. P. Feine, J. Behm, W.G. Kümmel, *Introduction to the New Testament*, 14th rev. ed., tr. by A.J. Mattill, Jr., (New York: Abingdon Press, 1966), p. 324.

2. (Philadelphia: Fortress, 1960).

3. (Philadelphia: Westminster, 1964).

4. SBT 2/22 (Naperville, Il.: Alec R. Allenson, 1972).

5. J. Massyngberde Ford, *Revelation: Introduction, Translation and Commentary* (Anchor Bible 38; Garden City, N.Y.: Doubleday, 1975).

6. Paul D. Hanson, *Revue Biblique* 78 (1971) p.31-58.

7. Hanson, *Interpretation* 25 (1971) pp. 454-479.

8. Hanson, (Philadelphia: Fortress Press, 1975), and Raymond Brown's review in the *Catholic Biblical Quarterly* 38 (1976) pp. 389-390.

9. Both definitions are found in P. Hanson, "Jewish Apocalyptic . . ." p. 35.

10. Feine-Behm-Kümmel, *op. cit.*, p. 318.

11. "The Political Perspective of the Revelation to John," *Journal of Biblical Literature* 96 (1977) p. 241.

12. The works of Fiorenza which are summarized here are: "The Eschatology and Composition of the Apocalypse," *Catholic Biblical Quarterly* 30 (1968) pp. 537-569; "Composition and Structure of the Revelation of John," *Catholic Biblical Quarterly* 39 (1977) pp. 367-381; and *The Apocalypse* (Chicago, Ill.: Franciscan Herald Press, 1976).

13. *The Gospel of Eternal Life*, (Milwaukee: Bruce Publ. Co., 1967) exp. pp. 146-170 on the Apocalypse.

14. Thierry Maertens and Jean Frisque, rev. ed. tr. by Molaise Meehan, (Notre Dame, Ind.: Fides Publishers, Inc., 1974), p. 54.